Permanent Adolescence

Permanent Adolescence
Why Boys Don't Grow Up

By
Joe Carmichiel, MSEd.

New Horizon Press
Far Hills, NJ

"On an Archaic Torso of Apollo" and "The Trains" are from *The Host: Selected Poems 1965-1990*, by William Heyen. Copyright © 1994 by Time Being Books. Reprinted by permission of Time Being Press.

"The Pigeons" is from *Pterodactyl Rose: Poems of Ecology*, by William Heyen. Copyright © 1991 by Time Being Books. Reprinted by permission of Time Being Press.

"Sea People" by Susan Astor is from *Silent Voices: Recent American Poems about Nature*, edited by Paul Feroe. Copyright © 1978 by Paul Feroe. Reprinted by permission of Paul Feroe.

"Ecstatic Love is an Ocean" by Rumi is from *The Winged Energy of Delight: Selected Translations, Poems from Europe, Asia and the Americas*, by Robert Bly. Copyright © 2005 by Robert Bly. Reprinted by permission of Robert Bly.

"A Ritual to Read to Each other" copyright © 1960, 1998 the estate of William Stafford. Reprinted from *The Way It Is* with the permission of Graywolf Press, Saint Paul, Minnesota.

Author's Note

All of the stories and vignettes in this book that are first person were derived from my real experiences as a classroom teacher in American high schools and middle schools. My interactions with male students were the foundation of my research and I tell their stories, because so many of these boys are in need of our help.

Real names, places and some minor material facts have been altered to protect the anonymity of the people in the stories. In order to protect privacy, fictitious names and identities have been given to all non-public individuals in this book and otherwise identifying characteristics have been changed.

Please visit http://www.PermanentAdolescence.com

Copyright remains with the original authors and/or publishers for all reprinted poems, stories, interviews and transcripts contained herein. "Thank you" to those authors. Please read their original works for more insight.

"Entering the Forbidden Room" first appeared on http://www.mensightmagazine.com/ in 2005

The information contained herein is not meant to be a substitute for professional evaluation and therapy.

Dedication

To Miriam, Natalie and Jackson

The greatest teachers I know

All over the world the faces
Of living ones are alike.

With tenderness they have
Come up out of the ground.

Look upon your children
That they may face the winds
And walk the good road to the Day of Quiet.

Grandfather Great Spirit
Fill us with the Light.
Give us the strength to understand,
And the eyes to see.

Teach us to walk the soft Earth
As relatives to all that lives.

Native American Prayer

As I have said, the irresistible tendency to account for
everything on physical grounds corresponds to the horizontal
development of consciousness in the last four centuries, and
this horizontal perspective is a reaction against the exclusively
vertical perspective of the Gothic Age.

Carl Jung

Table of Contents

Part III: Boys and Aggression

Acknowledgments

I began this project in 2005, while I was in my fifth year of teaching high school and middle school students. I had been noticing that many of my students appeared troubled, and I began to interview them, especially the boys, asking them what they were feeling, what they thought about their education, their peers, the adults in their life and their world. Their answers motivated me to dig deeper and work harder at this project, because I discovered there was something very wrong going on in American schools, and in the world beyond the school's walls, and it was harming our children, especially the boys, deeply. So, first and foremost, I want to thank my former students for allowing me to learn from them.

I would also like to thank my family, colleagues and many friends who supported me, assisted me and put up with me while I worked on this project. Some of these fine people are: Michael and Janet Barkun; Deborah Barkun and Jay Andrews; Mary and Sam Rotunda; Cathy McGowan and the staff of the Rhush-Rheese Library at the University of Rochester; teachers Jennifer Shultz, Brian Dastyck, Tim Padden, Connie Osborne, Linda Kimball, Sean O'Toole and Heather Uetz; graphic designer Erika Looney. Most importantly, I wish to thank my wife, Miriam, my daughter, Natalie, and my son, Jackson Neil, who was born during the writing of this book. They gave up a lot of me in order to make this project happen.

Introduction:
The Vertical Mind and
the Horizontal Mind

During my first year teaching high school, I found it difficult to persuade my students, especially the boys, to comply with my lesson plans and classroom rules. They gave me a lot of what I thought of at the time as "attitude"—teenage noncompliance. Observing this in my classroom, the school administrators sent someone to council me. His name was Jeff Linn, an experienced teacher and thoughtful friend. We had a talk in the school library one winter day, and I remember exactly what Jeff said to me: "Teaching is both an art and a science. The science is the subject you teach, putting commas in the right place or whatever it is. You have to know your stuff inside and out and I can't teach you that. But the other side of the coin is the art of teaching. The art of teaching has nothing to do with your subject area. It's not about English or Physics or Earth Science, it's about connecting with kids, understanding kids, relating to them. It's about knowing where they're coming from."

When I sat down to write this book about male adolescents and the influences and challenges modern culture has brought to their world, it became clear to me that Jeff's statement about art and science not only was true about teaching teenagers, but also was true about understanding their motivations in general, not just in a classroom. He had touched upon the key to bringing children into adulthood successfully: achieving the proper balance between the artistic mind and the scientific mind; forming the right balance between emotion and reason. I have become more aware in some cases, and newly aware in other cases, that the things influencing kids are both *artistic* and *scientific*. There's an art and a science to being a parent; there's an art and a science to being a kid; mostly, there's an art and a science to understanding our modern world. The factors that work on children's psyches, or souls, are as important, if not more important, than those things that work on the rational parts of their brains. While working in the classroom, I also began to notice that it was the literal, or "scientific," aspect of modern life—especially electronic media and consumer culture—that was coercing our children down a certain path. Their path, unfortunately, is a horizontal one, leading away from higher achievement, real growth and real potential. Our children are on a sideways path, not rising higher, not readying themselves to take on the challenges of the modern world. Children have come to look upon adulthood as their enemy, and they are doing all that is in their power to stay adolescents, many of them well into their so-called adult years.

A major problem with our post-industrial culture in the West is that we are relying almost exclusively on one part of the brain, one realm of thought and one domain of consciousness, both for building our educational systems and for relating to our children. The human brain does not work as a practical, scientific tool alone. It is a mind made up of two minds, the conscious and the subconscious, the artistic and the scientific, the physical and the metaphysical. The two realms must exist side by side and work in coalition if there is to be significant learning or development. Primary cultures have known and respected these two minds for centuries, and they have put the artistic, the mythological, the metaphysical, a faith in symbols, language and nature into every aspect of their lives, placing special importance on these issues when guiding their children, especially male children, into adulthood. There are countless examples of the rituals and myths primary cultures in North America,

Europe, Scandinavia, Africa, Indonesia, Australia and elsewhere have used to help their children succeed. Primary cultures all over the globe developed belief systems with mythological structures that were specifically meant to stimulate children's metaphysical development and to develop cohesion between the artistic and scientific parts of children's brains. These systems assisted young people through adolescence and helped convey a sense of place and the importance of nature and community, thus teaching the tribal values that would sustain them through their period of confusion and mistrust of adulthood and help them to recognize and assume their place in the world of adults.

Often in this book I'll refer to the practical, pragmatic, scientific mind as the "horizontal mind" and the artistic, metaphysical or intuitive mind as the "vertical mind." I like these terms—Carl Jung's terms—because the term vertical implies an upward movement, a progression, a movement seeking to achieve higher potential. Many cultures have cultivated the ability to address the development of the vertical mind for thousands of years. Knowledge in this realm falls under the heading of mythology, intuitiveness, occultism, religious knowledge, artistic sensibility, metaphysics or even what we might call the heart, the psyche, the soul or the spirit. It is the place where poets such as William Blake, psychologists and psychiatrists such as Carl Jung and artists such as Pablo Picasso dwelled.

The old system weighted its paradigm towards the mythological and away from the pragmatic. The human brain's development corresponded to this treatment by enlivening the physical structures in the brain where the subconscious does its work. These are the areas of the brain that dream, that connect to nature, that experience language and art and that reach out to others in a spiritual and experiential way. These are areas of the human brain that are buried deep within our mammalian core and that know, on some level, our ancient ancestors and our inherent relationship with the planet. Tribal peoples recognized the need to respect this part of the human mind and spirit. They developed a system to bring their children into adulthood by teaching them and allowing them to experience this respect, and it was a system that worked very well for millions of people over hundreds, likely thousands, of generations. It helped to successfully bring children into the fold of the adult structure, and it kept peace alive between peoples and between nature and people.

Each tribal band seemed to have its own particular mythology, symbolism and ritual structures, but most had strikingly similar focuses. For instance, the Luisenos Indians of Southern California used the Toloache Ceremony as a coming-of-age ritual for young men. They would mix a narcotic drink made from Jimsonweed that caused hallucinations and, in a controlled ceremonial setting with many comforting tribal elders present, induced the boys to take the potion. The boys had to fast in preparation for the ceremony, and it was built up through education for some time, much like a Bar Mitzvah is for young Jewish men today, in order to stress its relevance and importance. The Pueblos of the American Southwest had a Kiva Ceremony, similar in many respects to that of the Luisenos; the Hopis tribe held initiation ceremonies once a year for both male and female pubescent children. On the Great Plains, the tribes sent their adolescents on "vision quests" in order to help them achieve adult identities. Throughout South and Central America, Africa, Scandinavia, Australia and elsewhere, communities focused on raising their young with a respect for adulthood carved out of a background in mythological expression. All of these customs were developed for the same purposes, yet independently took on their own particular structures. They were part of a larger cultural plan to help young men and women through adolescence and form their identities around certain values.

These coming-of-age rituals, and their accompanying myths and symbols, were taking place with similar cultural importance in many other places around the globe in much the same way. So we know that tribal peoples all around the world knew that teenagers need a supportive mythological structure to successfully accomplish their transition into adulthood. They need a communal approach that respects the balance between the practical and the metaphysical. In fact, if we look at the development of these cultures, we see that they placed a high level of importance on this process that was tantamount to any other belief system. Their initiation process for young adults, especially boys, was as important as finding food, worshipping their gods or anything else, including survival itself. It seemed a given for many thousands of years that just as sure as there must be food, water and shelter, there must also be a mythological and ritualistic process, in addition to a teaching process consisting of practical skills such as hunting and farming, for helping adolescents become successful adults.

In modern day America, I feel we have done exactly the opposite from what primary cultures did and have come to believe exactly the opposite of what the tribal peoples took as a given throughout history. We have abandoned the coming-of-age process, de-emphasized the artistic mind and raced headlong with an unprecedented enthusiasm in a direction wholly opposed to mythology, tradition, ritual or any meaningful assistance for our children. We have chosen to force our kids to race towards adulthood, shoving sexuality, participation in the economic system, even adult language at them at the youngest ages ever, yet we are giving them little, if any, support in how to make sense of these adult symbols. The result is that we have created a generation of children who are rejecting adulthood altogether, as though it were an oppressive evil to be avoided at all costs.

If the artistic side of life is the knowledge of mythology, art, metaphysics, tradition and symbolic language as valued by the primary cultures, then we can say that the pragmatic or scientific side of life is the quest for wealth, technical achievement, mass production and dominance over one's environment. It has become the goal of modern education and, by default, the god of the modern world. We see it in every corner of our culture. Our children learn most of their language skills and cultural values from television programs instead of time spent with parents reading and talking. Instead of tribal associations, they build communities in internet chat rooms, e-mail exchanges or online gaming circles. Instead of the support of a community of elders, teens find their mentors in the movies, on television programs or flying through the air preparing to strike an opponent in a professional wrestling ring. A mountain of statistics proves that in the modern era, the American teenager and the American family have diminished significantly in qualitative and quantitative measures of stability and success. We know that boys are falling far behind girls in school; we know that language and communication skills across the genders, especially in boys, have weakened, and in some cases disappeared in young adults; we know that families with an adult male in the household are rare; we know that teenagers are increasingly turning to drugs, suicide, violence and many other measures of dysfunction; we know that many of our schools are in ruin and are failing to meet any meaningful standard. Could there be a connection between the failure of the American child and the abandonment of the artistic mind?

The electronic age, to be sure, has done much for our society, and it may be wrong to condemn it overall. However, we live in a world where our own creations, computers and electronics, television sets and MP3 players, have outgrown our ability to understand them. Living in a fully mechanized world has changed every dimension of how children learn, socialize and even how their brains develop. Many argue (and I'll discuss some of their ideas in later chapters) that watching television has caused changes in the evolutionary development of children's brains. To be sure, the electronic world has demonstrably destroyed the family system as we once thought of it. This has occurred, I believe, not because any one invention has become too popular or is too dangerous, but because as a culture we have changed the very nature of our collective minds. We have abandoned the world we should be exploring—the inner world of the psyche—and have embraced the outer world of consumerism, science, literalness and the paradigm that we can conquer all that resides in our world, or at least control it for economic purposes. We are seeing very clearly in the new millennium that our children are not a resource that we can mass-produce to our desired standards, regardless of how much we may believe in using a mechanical process to produce all that we desire.

Most disturbingly, the triumph of science over art, or as the famed psychoanalyst Carl Jung called it, the triumph of the horizontal mind over the vertical mind, has taken away both our desire and our ability to reach higher as a culture. Our heights and achievements are now measured by scientific and practical dimensions alone. Pick up any high school textbook that deals with modern American culture since World War II and it will list our communal accomplishments: Increases in the Gross Domestic Product, reduction in poverty and starvation, employment rates, and so on. But it will say nothing about the happiness of our children, the number of two parent families, international cooperation or domestic racial cohesion. It will say nothing about these qualitative measures, because they have all eroded significantly in the modern era. We see discovery today as a means for finding specific applications or products we can use. We no longer see discovery as a means of understanding ourselves and our world. Instead, we compliment ourselves for mapping the very blueprint of life—the human DNA strand—while at the same time our fathers are abandoning their children at record numbers, and those children are running down the street shooting one another, not feeling any remorse. Life has been reduced to a computer model with humanity little but an afterthought, all while we celebrate the defeat of the vertical mind (Jung called it the "vertical" mind, because it is the part of the human being with the most potential to rise up and develop into something more than it already is).

The negative implications of the electronic society are the most severe for children, especially boys. The dominance of the horizontal mind has eliminated children's abilities to accept the type of assistance they need to adequately develop into adults. It has also taken away adults' desire to support children with the necessary means. Better said, there is little desire on the part of adults to provide the rituals and traditions that have for all of history been the roadmap through adolescence, and children are no longer able to comprehend the importance of such rituals, thus discounting them and disdaining the world of adults altogether. Children no longer wish to join the adult world, many openly despise it, and they are increasingly remaining adolescent—in their behaviors, emotional maturity and relationship with the world. We have created a generation of men who are men in age alone, but are really still boys, emotionally detached, unaware of their psychic or spiritual dimension, unable to sustain meaningful relationships and incapable of performing meaningful roles in the world. We have created a generation of permanent adolescents, many of whom are now rising to leadership positions in our schools, businesses and government. They rush us to war, costing thousands of lives, cook the books at corporations so retirees cannot feed themselves and teach our children how to make as much money as possible regardless of how many people are harmed in the process.

There are few primary cultures left in the world that still practice traditional coming-of-age rituals. But those rituals and mythologies remain in the historical record, and some semblance of the practice still remains in different forms in different locations. Some cultures are even trying to reconstruct the ritual practices that have all but disappeared with the modern world. In researching these practices, I looked at some of the customs of primary peoples, such as the forest people of Borneo, various Native North American tribes, the coming-of-age practices of recent European-American settlers working in traditional agrarian systems and the myths of ancient Greece. I found that throughout history and across cultural boundaries the foundations of coming-of-age practices had been essentially the same. It was only while comparing all of human history to post industrial America and Europe did I find a significant change. Some of the information about these practices comes from literature, and this book will take a look at what Charles Dickens, the Ancient Greeks, Native Eskimos and other modern and ancient storytellers saw when they looked at the coming-of-age process in their cultures. So, at times, this book will read like literary analysis. At other times, we will travel deep into the developing brain of a child. We will examine their neurons and the development of the brain over time, and take a close look at the impact electronic media, especially television, has on children's brains. As this is a highly scientific topic (and I and probably the reader are by no means scientists), I will disseminate some of this information and try to make it more understandable. So, we will go together on a journey of discovery, trying to answer the basic question: Why are American children—especially boys—failing to meet their potential and suffering so deeply in the modern world? The journey will take us through issues in literature, psychology, anthropology, educational theory, history and several other disciplines. I hope we will, in the journey to come, reach an understanding of the central point: why American children are failing—failing to succeed in both artistic and scientific development. In particular, we will explore boys and why they are failing to progress to adulthood in a meaningful way and are failing to achieve their potential. In the twenty-first century, I believe we have turned back the clock on some important aspect of human development, not advanced it, and the reason is that we have abandoned traditional understandings of nature, learning and community in favor of a purely scientific paradigm.

Often, as you read, you may feel a sense of deep resignation and pessimism buried in these chapters. This, I think, comes from the fact that I do not believe that it is possible to return to many of the ways that will help us succeed as a culture. But these pessimisms are in the short term, probably because my thoughts have been formed as someone brought up in my time and place—the electronic age. We should keep in mind that humanity developed over many thousands, even millions, of years, as our scientific brains are well aware. The late conservationist, David Brower, often gave a speech in which he used the metaphor of a clock and a twenty-four hour day to represent evolutionary time. The big bang that created the universe was 12:00 and one second A.M.; single cell organisms crawled out of the primordial soup around 6:30 A.M.; the Pleistocene Era, with its megaflaura, giant mammals and stone age hunters, didn't happen until perhaps 9:30 P.M. or so. The industrial era, where electricity and the internal combustion engine have come to take over and bring about more change than in the entire twenty-four hours of the universe combined, is but a few seconds on that time clock—

about 11:59 P.M. If we think about time in this fashion, in Brower's evolutionary perspective, we might see our pessimism quite differently, because great change can happen in any direction in very short periods of evolutionary time. The clock of human development continues to tick away.

There has always been a vigorous debate among psychologists about the issue of nature versus nurture. Do children learn, progress and develop due to preprogrammed genetic maps, or is their development and outcome more a result of their environment, peers, household or education? There are schools of thought that reside on each side of this equation and a third that considers a blend to be the most likely answer. But there is a fourth option as well that is embedded in the question. What if nature and nurture were really not at all different, but one in the same? If we look at mythology this way—as being the combination of nature and nurture, the perfect blending of a natural, evolutionary process that fosters our preprogrammed human needs and supports them through environmental means—then we can begin to see its relevance. Mythical processes and their accompanying rites of passage serve both as an educational tool and as a pathway into a natural, psychic understanding of one's own being and nature. Put another way, instead of trying to teach to the artistic and scientific sides of the brain at the same time—a pedagogy that has failed miserably in the modern era—primary cultures found a way to combine both equators into a single unit. In fact, to many primary peoples there was no distinction at all between the inner world of aesthetics and intuition, what we might today call the psychic landscape, and the outer world of wine, wind, forest beasts, family and death. Even some of the primary words in the language of the ancient Greeks grew to have these understandings built into them. American linguist and folklorist Jeremiah Curtin wrote:

> Logos *grew to mean the inner constitution as well as the*
> *outward form of thought, and consequently became the*
> *expression of exact thought—which is exact, because it*

corresponds to universal and unchanging principles—and reached its highest exaltation by becoming not only the reason in man, but the reason in the universe...Mythos meant, in the wildest sense, anything uttered by the mouth of man...a story understood...True myths—and there are many such—are the most comprehensive and splendid statements of truth known to man.

As Curtain says, the "inner constitution as well as the outward form of thought" combined into something he calls "exact thought" and "truth." This seems important, because truth is not something that is generational or cultural. Truth is truth, and the main fact is that in our world, our modern physical and psychic landscape, our land of television and scientific achievement, we have the highest degree of deception of any culture at any time in human history. Not only is our thinking inexact, it is a downright perjury. The Greeks were but one culture—although an important one—who pursued the path to metaphysical, exact truth. They lived within its structures all the time. The world outside, that world of gods, nature and mythology, was their inner world as well. With no distinction, there was never a quandary or disagreement about "truth." Contrast this with the West in the twenty-first century and it is easy to see how far away from truth we have come, even though we spend so much cultural energy trying to achieve it. One can say that all the time spent disagreeing and bickering in the modern world, all the shoving matches in the school hallways, all the wanton destruction of our land, sea and air, all the guns and bombs of the Middle East, may be a result of the inner denial of this basic truth.

This concept seems difficult to grasp—the idea that all our outward problems may stem from nurturing one part of the mind while denying the needs of the other. But an understanding of this idea has tremendous implications for the field of education in the twenty-first century and beyond. We have heretofore subscribed to the notion that children need to learn in compartmentalized ways, first going to mathematics class in the morning, then Science, then English and so forth. We address the arts only if there is free time in their schedules, allowing music, drawing, welding and, of course, athletics. This educational notion speaks to the idea of multiple intelligences, a theory purporting that the child's brain is compartmentalized, much like a file cabinet. Mathematical knowledge is stored in one drawer, biology in another. One child's mathematics drawer may be very large compared to his ability to learn other disciplines, so we encourage him to go to college and become an accountant or engineer. Another child might have tremendous capacity for language. He might take advanced literature and writing courses, and his parents and teachers might encourage him to become a teacher or author. In modern schools, we have overstuffed the drawers dedicated to literal thinking, and we have locked the drawers where metaphysics reside.

Unfortunately, the compartmentalization view of education is deeply flawed, mostly because it ignores another realm of development and understanding, one that is very controversial and difficult to define. We might call this realm the "psyche." In the electronic age in which we live, even discussing a level of human understanding that cannot be scientifically measured is very dangerous. Often we simply discount any such discussion, and those who do discuss it are labeled as crackpots or occultists. We are programmed to discount this realm because we are taught from a very young age that the only knowledge that is worthy of consideration is that which we can justify with data, or at least with deeply researched and documented literal understandings and scientific data. But the development of the brain's ability to *know* something about the world without having to analyze it in a linear, application-oriented way is very important. Deep down, most of us realize the importance of the psychic realm, but few of us are willing to risk an open belief in it as being more important than our science. Many are afraid to acknowledge its importance as equal to that of the scientific side, other than in our religious observances, which I'll argue later is really just horizontal mindedness as well. Least of all, we would never consider placing anything remotely vertical in our educational systems, which are judged so rigorously and measured so scientifically. What we do know, however, is that primary cultures founded their beliefs and cultural systems in the area of vertical thought, or the part of the person we can think of as the spiritual or artistic part. In the modern, electronic era, we have not only bastardized these beliefs, but we have wholly abandoned them in most cases.

What we are left with, in this post-mythological era, is an empire whose domination over the natural world is all but complete. That is to say, as a society we feel as though we have conquered not only nature, but also have asserted our dominance over societal organization and all of its entities: education, family structure, government and economics. Modernity itself has come to be defined by practical human domination over all else. We have also determined that we have conquered the inner landscape, generating pills to treat everything from fatigue to schizophrenia. The resulting dogmatic view resists any entreat from the old view, that the vertical mind may be worthy of development, and thus it stomps out any attempt to persevere in spiritual directions. Our scientific paradigm ignores the fuel for vertical growth, thus extending the horizontal plane further and further out toward the horizon. This is a dangerous situation. We have taken one entire realm of human understanding and not only put it on the stove's back burner, but also stuffed it in the oven, doused it with gasoline and are attempting to completely incinerate it.

There are many statistics that show how troubled our culture is. Most of us know this to be fact on an intuitive or experiential level. Most of us deal with the problems of the horizontal world on a daily basis, in our jobs and in our families. Even driving down the street we smell the smog, become frustrated over the traffic and hear the horns, sneers and anger of other drivers. We see violence expanding exponentially in America and globally, and the world's resentment of American culture is growing by leaps and bounds. We see many countries lining up to oppose America and its partners due to a perceived arrogance and because we are seen as a practical and symbolic threat to the successful traditions that have carried other cultures through time. At present, this conflict is manifested daily in the Middle East and the Islamic world's growing opposition to Western cultural influence. In America, we see our marriages failing and our children growing resentful. All around us people young and old are turning to drugs and alcohol in order to cope with modern life. Violence has become an everyday occurrence in many schools and in many neighborhoods. Our children, more than our own generation or the generations before, seem more mistrusting of the world around them and less optimistic than ever before. Ellen McGrath notes in a *Psychology Today* newsletter on teen depression that one in three teenagers will "end up with significant clinical depression needing treatment." What was once adolescent consternation is now defined resignation. Our immense frustration as a society is omnipresent, and it is a characteristic that pervades most aspects of our lives.

Violence in all forms is rampant in our cities, with a disturbing trend of increasing viciousness being committed by young boys. Prisons are bursting at the seams. Presently, according to the United States Department of Justice, there are over two million people in prisons and jails in America, a number that has grown annually at a rate of 2 to 3 percent for the last ten years. I believe the American family is functioning at its lowest levels ever. In the black community, approximately 65 percent of children are raised without a father in the household. In the white community, the number is closer to 35 percent, and both are increasing. The economic systems to which we subscribe keep very large percentages of the population in poverty so severe that every aspect of their lives is troubled, from nutrition and healthcare to educational expectations and survival. Real wages in America have not increased since the 1970s, and the once-prosperous and comfortable middle class has all but disappeared. As of the 2006 census, there are 32.9 million Americans living in poverty, and over 16 percent of all American children now live below the poverty level. We know that the poverty level is so extreme that living moderately above it is barely surviving, or not surviving at all (for example, the defined poverty level for a family of four in the contiguous United States is $18,850.00. But feeding and housing a family of four with that income ensures suffering, malnutrition, poor or nonexistent medical and dental care, unsafe housing and a host of other complications).

We will take a journey in this book through the world of our sons—the ways in which their brains develop as infants, the things they watch on television, the people they interact with at school—and we will see a disposition towards violence, a trend away from literacy and an overall resignation in modern youth culture that can, in part, be traced back to our abandonment of traditional coming-of-age practices and our cultural embrace of the horizontal mind.

In this horizontal world where the worlds of television and popular culture dominate the child's landscape, boys seem to be hurting the most. Their academic achievement is much lower than girls, their rates of incarceration and violence are growing steeply and their fathers are abandoning them en masse. Many boys are becoming permanent adolescents who never learn to progress beyond childhood, never strive to reach higher than the comforts of popular culture and have no concept of the potential they are missing out on. Worse, they are becoming the fathers of the next generation—a generation whose problems are bound to be exponential, unless we can assume some responsibility for these errors and begin to correct them.

Part ①

Stuck in Adolescence

①

Contempt for Grown-ups

Permanent adolescence occurs when a boy fails to progress to manhood in any meaningful psychic or emotional way. Our culture extends adolescence, both by design and by consequence of its industrial and electronic expansion. In the modern era, we have developed a worship of the physical state of youth. As we see on television, hour by hour, and as we have seen in advertisements for many years, the youthful ideal is placed before us as the supreme replica of perfection. The face and torso of Ashton Kutcher has replaced the bust of Apollo for our culture. Whether it is the face of the teenage model in clothing commercials or the sports all-star pitching long-distance telephone service, it is the youthful ethos that drives modern popular culture. A large number of today's teenagers, especially boys, see no reason to accept or pursue adulthood since it is of so little value to the larger culture.

Aside from the physical state of youth that our culture worships in media, the emotional side of youth is idealized as well. We see all around us young, middle-aged and even older men unemployed or underemployed, because of an emotional detachment from commitment and responsibility. Some drink too much alcohol, decline long-term relationships and play video games in the basement for hours on end.

We all know of such men, twenty-, thirty- and forty-year-olds, who are not really men at all, but rather aging children caught in a trance-like state void of adult responsibility...a place we can call *Permanent Adolescence*. Near the schools at which I have taught, I see young men in their mid to late twenties socializing on the playgrounds with fifteen- and sixteen-year-olds: skateboarding with them after school, dating the young girls, immersing themselves in teen culture. These twenty-somethings see adolescents and even pre-adolescents as their peer group, because they are emotionally at the same developmental stage and, without meaningful assistance, they will likely never progress beyond it. Instead of heading off to college, to monogamous family life, or to a career, these young men are heading over to their teenage peer group after school hours to play the latest video games and giggle, much like they did five, ten or fifteen years earlier while in high school.

Some permanent male adolescents choose not to socialize with teenagers, but behave as such when possible. Such men may maintain a job where they have some level of responsibility, but as their free time permits, they retreat to the basement to play games, surf the internet or obsess over the latest fantasy sports draft. Their endeavors are driven by an overemphasis on popular culture and motivated by an immature focus on identity definition—a process that should have been completed many years before. Their lives often center around artificial interests that have little meaning. Their deepest level of emotional attachment may be to a pet, a favorite sports team, even a favorite television show or computer game. Such men may even maintain marriages or long-term relationships, but these are often troubled, with wives or partners who understandably feel abandoned and children who feel the despair of an absent father living right in the same household with them. It is not that these men have consciously chosen to forgo committed family life, spiritual commitment or dedication to a career; instead, they are simply living at their developmental level. When their significant other complains that they are neglecting their family duties, they may wonder, "What's her problem? Doesn't she get how important fantasy baseball is?" Just like the teenager who cannot distinguish between the temptation of socializing with peers and the responsibility of doing schoolwork, these men are unable to comprehend the demands and sacrifices of adult life. They are adult in age alone, but psychically, emotionally and spiritually, they remain adolescent.

Many adult men in America, while perhaps not being full-fledged permanent adolescents, are showing some of the traits of emotional immaturity and rejection of adult responsibility. Their relationships with other men center around drinking alcohol and talking in a misogynistic tone about women, or they simply use social relationships to avoid real commitment in some other aspect of their life. In the eyes of their family they are "underachievers," but their real deficiency is not as simple as laziness. Often, their lives are a result of modeling the adolescent traits they learned as youths; traits that feel comfortable but keep them, on some level, adolescents. People in the adult world who perceive this adolescent character do not recognize it for exactly what it is, but know that the man before them is not one of them. Thus the adult world shuns the permanent adolescent to some extent, further preventing any emotional development.

We do not see the same trend in women, at least to the same degree. Of course, there are women who abandon their adult responsibilities or decline to ever accept them, and I have met some mothers of this type in my role as a teacher. Typically, these are mothers who are no longer able to care for their children, because the children have become uncontrollable, their lives are too crowded with drugs and alcohol or they are struggling with one of the many omnipresent obstacles modern life presents. I usually meet these mothers when they are either beginning a difficult period that will require change in the child's household or entering situations that are causing their children to struggle in school. Occasionally I meet them when they are returning to a child's life after a period of absence—coming back from a year living with a boyfriend out of town or exiting a substance abuse program or incarceration. Often, the children have been staying with other relatives while "Mom has been out of the picture." The difference between these women and the fathers I meet struggling with permanent adolescence is that almost without exception the mothers feel and express a genuine sense of remorse and ownership for their absence. Moreover, they seem able to confront their choices, in some cases overcome them, but even if not, they are, as a group, still able to understand their problem, whatever it may be, and understand that it is not their identity. There is a certain dignity, even nobility, in their demeanor, because no matter the challenge, they never seem to lose their identity as mothers. The men entranced by permanent adolescence are equally debilitated, but have no understanding that this is a period in their lives that might, with further education, the right choices or proper assistance, be conquered and left in their past. It is simply who they are. They feel indignation that people are challenging them about their lifestyles, mainly because they see nothing unusual about them. They are unable to separate their identities as adolescents from their identities as parents.

The sons of permanent adolescents typically have little or no respect for adults or the adult world in which they live and attend school. For there is a multigenerational trend developing in America in terms of permanent adolescence and the growing dislike for adulthood is the result. I see many families struggling with this phenomenon in my work as a teacher. One family that I have dealt with in my former school district was typical of this situation. The son, Jim, had acted badly in school for some time. He disregarded teachers and the principal, told adults who tried to moderate his behavior to "fuck off," ignored the school rules of dress code, classroom behavior and drug possession, and generally was insubordinate. His disrespect for adults was palpable. Various teachers and school officials tried to contact Jim's father, Tom, who had sole custody of his son, but the father did not return phone calls. Tom was spending most of his time at a local tavern. At school, Jim was respected and envied by his peers for having such an unstructured home life and for his boldness. Tom slept until noon and then indulged his alcoholism at the taverns until late evening. Tom rarely saw his son and communicated with the world outside the tavern culture even less. By the time the situation became so severe that the son was about to be removed from the school permanently, a meeting was finally arranged with Tom. He arrived sober and coherent. But when the teachers, counselors and administrators detailed his son's disobedience and complete defiance of the school's rules, the father became genuinely annoyed and bewildered. "I don't get it," he said. "Just because Jim told a few teachers to go screw themselves you want to throw him out of school? Are you people crazy?"

The father in this story had deep contempt for the adult world. Tom saw nothing wrong with disobeying the rules and codes of adulthood, because he himself had never experienced adulthood, even though he was over forty years old. He could see no reason to assist with his son's compliance of a culture that was as foreign to him as a tribe from the Amazon rainforest.

Economic challenges for adults in the industrial era make adulthood less than desirable. The competitive nature of global economic systems has created a stressed-out and overworked population in America and many other countries. Even jobs once thought to be "unskilled" now require years of advanced education or apprenticeship. The typical physician coming out of medical school in the United States has attended college for at least six years and is over $90,000 in debt, says Jennifer Proctor in her *AAMC Reporter* article "Medical School Debt." Many youths see adulthood as only an opportunity for bone-grinding work, uncontrollable debt and a life of little enjoyment. There is a fallacy that was once successfully sold to the post-war generations that said if one worked hard enough, a comfortable living could be had. Youths today realize that hard work can be much less satisfying and that the rewards are by no means guaranteed. For many teenage boys, their economic role models are the highly-stylized icons created by the media. Superstar athletes like LeBron James, music stars like 50 Cent and actors like Shia LaBeouf gain tremendous wealth while doing what they have always done: playing ball, singing or acting. There is little reason to pursue the economic justifications of the adult world when the comfort of permanent adolescence is so available, so inexpensive and so widely supported, not to mention that being a regular teenager might just pay off in wealth and stardom.

Men stuck in permanent adolescence feel a genuine contempt for adult culture, but they are often not mature enough to make sense of the reasons, and so remain in a seesaw existence between anger and precociousness. The Greeks recognized some of this in their own and developed the god Hermes to help explain it. Hermes was born to Zeus—the supreme ruler of the universe. But Hermes was born of an extramarital affair with a mortal and thus never quite fit in. From the beginning, Hermes was something of a prankster. The baby Hermes, as a two-day-old, was already wandering away from his cave and mother. On his first foray, he found some of Apollo's cattle and took them. His naughtiness landed him in trouble with the adults, but he had little concern for them. His righteousness was so prevalent that he was unable to understand anything of his own failings. When his mother asked him why he had stolen the cattle, he told her that he wished to make a sacrifice to the *twelve* Olympian Gods. "Twelve?" asked his mother, perplexed. There had until that time only been eleven. "I'm going to be the twelfth!" Hermes arrogantly announced.

The arrogance of adolescence, whether it is displayed in adults or in children, is much like Hermes'. Neither recognize their shortcomings and both envision a world of "others" seeking to repress or corral their natural—and godly—instincts for self-indulgence. Hermes was born after Zeus secretly impregnated Maia. Neither Maia nor Zeus ever fully accepted Hermes. He was part god and part human, the least of both worlds. Adult adolescents, in the same way, feel especially disconnected from their mothers and fathers. They may still rely on their mothers for many comforts, not the least of which may be meals and laundry, but they are often in an emotionally distant state from them. Moreover, their fathers, like Zeus, do not welcome paternity and may either reject the adolescent, because of their sheer lack of compliance with parental expectations or have rejected the child long ago for other reasons, perhaps engendering the lack of emotional progress.

In teenage boys there is always the chance—in some cases even the probability—that given enough time, or enough stimuli (college, the military, getting a job, positive adult role models), that they will make the progression to adulthood in some sort of leap. We see it many times in high school children. The boy leaves at the end of the school year as an immature, frazzled wreck and returns in September four inches taller, twenty pounds heavier and with the ability to articulate his intelligence like an adult. "I can't believe how he's changed," the teachers say. But the adult adolescent cannot make this leap, for he has missed the window of opportunity long ago. Any change will be modest, if at all, and little can be expected.

Mothers and Sons

One factor in the onset of permanent adolescence is that boys who never progress into emotional manhood are often the children of single parent homes without fathers or of homes with domineering or abusive fathers. Their boyhoods are spent in the role of mother protectors, not because their mothers place this role upon them or do anything wrong, but because they themselves feel the need to protect their mothers' virtue and emotional well-being from adult men. The feeling that they must become protectors happens because there is no strong or positive adult males present in their home lives. If there is an adult male in the home, he may have the persona of a domineering patriarch, yelling commands, terrorizing the household or ruling what he perceives as his kingdom through tyranny. Such boys spend much of their adolescence as a sentry, either physically or, more likely, in a fantasy where they envision themselves as the "man of the house." Adolescent boys may take on the role of protector if their father dies or because he is weak, alcoholic or otherwise absent from the household, not just because their father is abusive. In either case, there is a void where the *real* father, the strong father, should be. Instead, there is a tyrant, or no one at all.

The problem for such boys is that instead of learning the emotional lessons of adolescence from male role models, they are on duty. Their self-appointed jobs as sentries are very serious to them and take on military importance in their lives. Their sense of duty prevents them from taking the time necessary or having the initiation experiences necessary to move through adolescence successfully and develop the emotional skills they need to achieve successful transitions to adulthood.

Men like Elvis Presley, pop singer Michael Jackson and former president Bill Clinton are good examples of men in popular culture who took on the sentry role as adolescents and failed to progress emotionally. Presley, as many biographers have noted, had strong attachments to his mother and fancied himself his mother's protector. As an adult, the women in his life were measured by a mother standard none could meet. His life, music and stage presence were over-sexualized, and he never progressed emotionally beyond the point of a fifteen- or sixteen-year-old.

Likewise, Jackson's domineering and allegedly abusive father placed him in the sentry role as a child. But children are rarely able to actually protect themselves or anyone else from a domineering patriarch. Physically they are weak and emotionally they are inexperienced. Sometimes the anger and resentment builds throughout childhood and into adolescence until their minds and bodies catch up with their anger and resentment and violence erupts. Other times, the sentry realizes the futility of his position and runs away, joins the military at the first opportunity, or otherwise exits the physical and emotional household.

Bill Clinton had a similar experience. But in his case, his role as sentry was more real than fantasy. He grew up in an abusive household, much of it stemming from his stepfather and directed at his mother. Clinton assumed the role of mother protector and grew up to risk the most prominent career in the world by having extramarital relations with a young woman in the White House.

The Ancient Greeks had something to say about this phenomenon as well. The story of Odysseus' travels is a good example. Telemachus, Odysseus' son, takes on the role of mother protector while his father is away on his odyssey. He does what he can to keep order in the castle, protect his mother, Penelope, from evil suitors, and search for his missing father. But the Greeks wisely created Penelope as a strong and independent wife and mother. She protects the kingdom of Ithaca from the dastardly suitors as well, even creating a deception that keeps them occupied for some time until Odysseus returns. Telemachus never has to live as an adult with the burden of a failed sentry on his shoulders, because his father, unlike many in our culture, returns and fulfills his role.

The phenomenon of permanent adolescence has arisen in recent years for many reasons. Rapid changes in the family, for example, have come upon us in the industrial and post-industrial era. The lack of emotionally present fathers in the home has certainly changed the ways sons and daughters relate to the world. Additionally, these factors have motivated children to chisel their expectations and admiration of adults. Given a poor or nonexistent model, what child would want to aspire to his maternal or paternal example?

②

The Brain and
Electronic Culture

A bove and beyond behavioral influences, there may be changes occurring in the neocortex and developmental processes of the human brain due to the electronic culture. This may mean that permanent adolescence is causing changes in evolutionary brain development, which are curbing our society's ability to reach higher levels scientifically and artistically and, as some have argued, may have even put an end to the brain's evolution as we have known it. We are now learning more about the developmental changes in the brain that take place during adolescence.

The progression of advanced reasoning skills, hypothetical thinking and meta-cognitive processes are developmental traits of early, mid and late adolescence. During this time, kids develop the ability to realize how others perceive them and how they should perceive others. They also develop mnemonic devices that help them learn and prosper academically. It is these particular developmental processes, and their connected structures in the brain that may be anesthetized to a point of uselessness or underdeveloped to a point of ineffectiveness because of interaction with television, computers and other electronic media.

Most people assume that the human brain has unlimited potential for evolutionary development. Weighing in at a mere three to four pounds, the brain contains somewhere in the neighborhood of eleven *billion* specialized nerve cells, or neurons, that interpret and help us interact with the emotional, spiritual and physical world, defining what we call reality. Not only the sheer number, but also the organization and connectivity of the neurons are what shape our evolutionary development. Evolutionary changes in the human brain occur in spurts, or blooms, as scientists call them, and it only took a relatively small number of changes to make us *human* in the twenty-first century electronic age, instead of *human* in the Paleolithic, cave dweller variety. After all, both are the same species. In fact, the current variety of humans share over 98 percent of the exact DNA as the common chimpanzee. Small changes in the brain's evolution can make a big difference.

To help us understand evolution in the brain, let's compare the brain's neurons to a willow bush. The neuron is the core appliance, thicker, stiffer and central to that part of the brain's activity. But stemming off of the willow bush are many smaller, wiry branches. In the brain, these are called dendrites and they act much like antennae, sending out and intercepting communication from other neural clusters. These antennae activate when they are stimulated in certain ways; they even change their polarity, depending on whether they are at that moment sending or receiving signals. One of the most amazing things about these structures is their ability to communicate over long distances. But the neurons in the brain must be connected in order to communicate. It is more like a telegraph system from the turn of the century than the cell phone systems we use today to call across the country. The lines connecting neurons are called synapses, and they do extend, but not all that far. We might say that a willow bush in Manhattan could probably call over to Long Island, but would be hard pressed to reach Kansas or even Philadelphia. For this reason, evolutionary development in the brain happens regionally, and regions of the brain almost always have interconnected synonymous applications such as language, reasoning, visual processing or any number of other functions.

Research has shown that single sensory stimuli can change the communication signals sent by the neurons. Scientists call this phenomenon *plasticity*. It refers to the brain's ability to adapt itself and change its neural structures to meet environmental needs and respond to environmental changes. Brain researchers are thus faced with a single, perplexing question: How did the brain develop the ability to answer complex scientific questions, make astounding engineering and technological advancements and almost completely subdue the natural environment in a couple of hundred years when these issues were not even minimally addressed in the thousands of years preceding? Did the brain have a sort of evolutionary growth spurt, or was this all simple happenstance that occurred because the same brain structures, which had always existed, suddenly came together in the right time and the right place, as though a certain divine coalition had been arranged? We've talked previously about the differences and similarities in the scientific brain and the intuitive, or artistic, part of the brain. Few would dispute that with all of the advances in science and technology that developed over a very short evolutionary span, it is the scientific areas of the brain that have won in the modern race for evolutionary development. The changes have been substantial, to say the least, in recent times.

Another possibility is that the progression in the brain's structures in the areas of science and technology occurred as an unintended result of basic evolutionary development for survival. We know that the first computers were developed to calculate spreadsheets and handle financial data in the banking industry. But later, those same computers were found to be able to operate word processing, games, and, a few short decades later, the internet and other communication activities. The brain's development, we should consider, may have happened much the same way. It may have been the reasoning areas of the brain that changed slightly, perhaps for some agrarian purpose. Maybe the brain needed someone to figure out how to build irrigation systems, for example, in order to provide a better harvest. But the unintended result was the ability to reason and invent too well—and a few hundred or thousand years later, we have a world with six hundred million motor vehicles and enough nuclear weaponry to destroy the earth fifty times over. We should note here that the theory of unintended evolutionary results was developed by American evolutionary paleontologist Stephen Jay Gould. He gave the phenomenon the name *exaptation*, and wondered, "How much of the evolutionary literature on human behavior would collapse if we incorporated the principle of *exaptation* into the core of our evolutionary thinking?" Gould considered many of the human brain's abilities to be accidental side effects of other, more purposeful evolutionary developments.

It could be that the brain's development over time was intended to be in the realm of intuition, metaphysics, relationship building or emotional determination. It could be that humans were on their way to becoming artists, or that we were meant to be a complex web of peaceful tribes that had unique sensibilities about their relationships with nature. We might have been heading towards a true higher consciousness, one that may have resulted in the ideals of some sixties radicals coming to fruition: world peace, higher love, artistic genius, no more hunger, no more war, no more destruction. We might, in fact, if Gould is correct, have those potentials already developed within us, but instead are using them for other means, such as acquiring wealth and expanding democracy. We may have evolved to become magically divine and harmonious, but ended up hostile and self-destructive. A few neuron clusters can make quite a difference.

In the electronic age, moreover, we have given rise to stimuli that affect brain development and, consequently, brain evolution, in unfathomable ways. It has been long established that the brain develops or kills certain structures very quickly in response to stimuli. Nobel Prize winners David Hubel and Torsten Wiesel discovered this phenomenon in the 1970s by experimenting on cats. Their noteworthy experiments included one in which they forcibly closed one eyelid of a newborn cat. They found that in only one week, the axons carrying nerve signals from the closed eye were barely developing, whereas the connections from the open eye were developing at a faster than normal rate. When the cat's sewn-shut eye was later opened, it had permanently lost the ability to see. Hubel and Wiesel's experiments essentially show that neurons in the brain compete with one another based upon sensory stimuli. One can imagine neuron pathways in the brain trying to compete for development in the language centers. Electronic media, namely televisions and computers, have some of the most powerful stimulating effects on the brain known to humankind. In the war for dominance between television and books, we know which stimulus is winning the battle for neural growth.

It is known that human brain development happens in spurts or developmental windows, which occur in condensed time periods during childhood, many of them before age three. Researcher Peter Huttenlocher of the University of Chicago looked at the brains of people who had died at various ages, missing the opportunity for certain developmental windows, and counted and compared the synapses of various parts of the brain. He found that by age two synaptic density is at its maximum, and by adolescence only about 60 percent of the brain's original synaptic connections are still present. The brain seems to develop and then shed the structures that are not suitable for adulthood, much like a florist picking through a bouquet of flowers and discarding the wilted and off-color blooms. This tells us that the critical developmental periods for the brain occur before age three, the time when the brain is most susceptible to the damage of electronic stimuli such as television. It may be that because we rely so much upon electronic media to help raise our children, we are only permitting our children's brains to develop a small vase of ragweed and dandelion instead of an enormous bouquet of red, pink and yellow roses, wildly-colored lilies, sunflowers and African violets.

The main ingredient that is training our brains to think horizontally and ruining our ability to work aesthetically, I believe, is the technology culture in which we live. Television and dozens of other electronic devices, which our world is now so predicated upon, have an underlying message. They preach by their very existence that scientific thought—the production of machines to better our lives—is the purpose of life; they tell us to buy more and build more; and they tell us that anything organic is outdated, unnecessary and downright subhuman.

Since evolution is a slow process, it may take dozens or even thousands of generations before we understand the impact of this change in any meaningful way. Evolution is an organic process. But man-made development is exactly the opposite: it takes place quickly, without much forethought or trial and error, and with fewer checks and balances than were once provided by conceptual blending. Man-made development has now taken over the processes that evolution developed for bringing children into adulthood successfully. The developmental windows in early childhood and adolescence are now dominated by man-made forces such as television, and we are now beginning to see exactly how detrimental reliance upon inorganic forces can be.

We are learning that our minds do not operate like computers. Thinking does not happen in algorithms, nor does any type of higher-level thinking occur outside the coalition of emotion, reason, prior experience, future expectation, cultural example and biological consequence. We know that to think in grand terms, to explore new horizons and to make true progress toward achieving human potential, we must incorporate the figurative with the literal; the artistic with the scientific; the vertical with the horizontal.

Thus, we have a problem when one way of thinking becomes too dominant. In our time, the economic and cultural landscape has changed. The literal mind has become so powerful that the artistic mind is in danger of dying out. We see the consequences of this trend: the decrease in reading and writing scores on standardized tests; the failure of the family; the increases in violence and our children's normalization of it; the lowering of almost all standards of what was once considered civilized behavior; the young rebelling in a new way—instead of reacting against the adult community, they are resolving to abstain from it altogether.

Politically, many of us now lack the will to help address the suffering of other nations. The thousands dying today in refugee camps in Darfur and other such places no longer resonate with too many minds. Many lack the will to care deeply for other people, because we can no longer feel their suffering, experience their pain or empathize on a figurative level. Because we cannot see life as symbols or detect deeper meaning on figurative levels, our decisions are based upon a very different set of criteria than in generations past. Take, for example, a light switch. We might consider our actions very differently if, when we flipped on the light switch in our home, we saw the smokestacks at the local power plant spewing pollution and heard the screams of the two-year-old in the hospital's pediatric cancer ward suffering from tumors caused by the power plant's pollution. It is a very different set of considerations than if we see flipping a light switch as simply switching on the lights. The same is true for stories. If the Greek's Oedipus story, for example, was only applicable to Oedipus and not to anyone else in the future, then an entire field of psychology has been nullified. We can say the same for much of the research that has taken place over the past one hundred years. What good is knowledge if we cannot apply it in metaphorical context?

Our children seem to be suffering the most. They seem to sense that something is wrong with the adult world. What was once a culture that raised its young by providing solid role models, supportive stories and carefully constructed coming-of-age rituals now hurl children to the adult world without much support. The children look at the adults and see deprivation. They see divorced parents, neglected children, schools that fail them on every level and an economic system that is built on greed instead of humanity. Their stories, instead of providing a positive picture of life ahead and lessons on how to get there, are told by television programs focusing on violence, intolerance and a set of moral values that is nothing short of horrific. These stories, and those from other questionable sources such as video games, popular music, computers, etc., have become the primary teachers of our young. They do not promote aesthetic blending in any way; they promote pseudo scientific homogeny. Increasingly, teenagers, especially boys, are rejecting their invitation into the adult world altogether, remaining instead in a state of permanent adolescence. They reject the former values of the adult world. They also fail to culturally innovate, maintain successful relationships and bring new knowledge into the world. And ultimately, they fail when they become parents themselves. It is a fact of the horizontal mind that once it achieves dominance, it remains firmly in control and is self-perpetuating.

In a horizontal world, we do not look to the past for stories that can explain our present. Nor do we look to the future to understand the consequences of our actions, because we have lost the ability to project our thoughts metaphorically into the future. We only consider the present, which often is presented to us in glamorous, sanitized pictures on the television screen. In reality, the stories we see on television are not like the stories from mythology or from the great works of literature. They are condensed to fit into specific time slots, and their medium in and of itself is fictional and destructive.

③

Media and Boys' Minds

Another consequence of television is the connection between watching television during childhood and the onset of Attention Deficit Hyperactivity Disorder (ADHD) and Attention Deficit Disorder (ADD). As I mentioned earlier, I have witnessed an increase in the number of children, especially boys, exhibiting attention disorder and hyperactivity in the classroom in recent years. Some of my own classes have had as many as four or five students who cannot sit still, pay attention to simple instructions or even remain in their seats for more than a few minutes at a time without acting out with uncontrollable energy. I am only aware of the ones I observe who are not being treated. There are more, I am sure, who are sitting in their seats with controlled ADHD. However, even one student with uncontrolled ADHD in a class of twenty-five can disrupt the learning for the entire class; imagine what happens when there are four or five such students in the room.

Michael, an eighth grader in one of my classes, was constantly physically active while in the classroom. When he was forced to sit in his seat, he reacted as though he were a caged animal, whirling around in his chair, tapping his hands and fingers on the desk or taking off his shoes and kicking desks and students in front of him. It came to a point where any student who was seated near him begged to be moved, until there were no longer any places in the classroom to move desks, since Michael needed a good five-foot radius of open space between him and anything that would become an object of interaction. If he sat near the computer, he would invariably play with the switches and keyboard; if he sat near my desk, he would open and close the drawers; if he sat near another student, he would play footsie with them. Several times I was in a different part of the room and glanced over at Michael. At those times, he often pulled his arms back behind him and banged his head over and over again on the desktop until a round, reddish circle appeared on his forehead. When I spoke with Michael about his misbehavior, he said, "I can control it. I'll try harder." Students today like Michael are common in America's classrooms and are not so quietly diminishing the overall population's ability to learn.

Research studies have shown a clear connection between watching television during the infant or toddler stages and later developing symptoms of ADHD. In the April 2004 issue of the journal *Pediatrics*, Dr. Dimitri A. Christakis, Director of the Child Health Institute at Children's Hospital and Regional Medical Center in Seattle and under the auspices of the American Academy of Pediatrics, published a study that reverberated throughout the country. The study showed that watching television causes a higher probability of developing ADHD and that the greater the amount of time spent watching (and listening to) television during the critical developmental years up to age three, the greater the likelihood of developing symptoms of the disorder. Dr. Christakis and his team argued that watching television during the years when the language and learning centers of the brain are forming essentially "rewires" the brain. The damage shows up beginning around age seven.

Dr. Christakis argues—and his study has been backed by brain scans at leading institutions such as the Amen clinic—that the brain's language areas need certain types of organic stimulation in order to develop during youth. But with so much of the child's time spent watching television, the brain does not have the opportunity to interact with the complexities of environmental stimulation it needs in order to develop fully. For example, the sound spectrum is immensely diverse. Sound has both decibel levels and pressure gradients, not to mention the fine nuances of tone. With these attributes, there are literally millions of different sound combinations, from the pitter-patter of raindrops on a window, to the screech of a jackhammer on the city streets, to the caw of a raven in a tree. These sound combinations react in the brain both physically, through pressure, and emotionally, by tapping into corresponding internal databases of prior knowledge and experiences. Such interaction with sound is the organic phenomenon the brain responds to by developing neural circuitry to interpret it. But the passive sound that comes from the television set is nothing like the organic sounds we hear in real life. Its spectrum is so thinly prescribed that all television sounds can be measured in approximately $1/1000^{th}$ of the overall sound spectrum found in nature. By hearing noise that is both meaningless and also non-diversified, the brain has no need to develop neural pathways for interpretation.

As observers, we can look at this phenomenon from both the scientific and the intuitive sides of our brains. For instance, we know that on television, and especially in children's programming, the pace of information delivery is sped up. There are quick scene shifts, snappy music, characters running and jumping, often in groups, and many chases, playful fights (some not so playful) and animals chasing one another through the jungle, across the desert and swimming in the ocean. When I was a child, I watched the *Road Runner* cartoon, with the speedy bird constantly on the run from that demented coyote and his anvils and dynamite. My daughter's generation is much more likely to watch one of the Walt Disney movies such as *Finding Nemo*, where a cute and colorful fish is constantly avoiding shark attacks, divers and other perils; or *Madagascar*, where lions are constantly hunting burrowing beasts and penguins attack a container ship's crew and steer it to the Antarctic. The content of these programs aside, it is the pace of the information flow that is problematic to the developing brain. Life does not happen at the speed depicted in children's television and movies. Thus, the child's brain becomes used to seeing and understanding life at a hyperspeed. The brain circuitry, which develops very quickly at this age, arises around an environment of super-speed imagery. This over-stimulation causes permanent, irreversible changes in the neural pathways in a child's brain.

Dr. Christakis further supports his study of the connection between watching television and the onset of ADHD with the U.S. Department of Labor's National Longitudinal Survey of Youth. This survey researched over two thousand kids. It noted that for every hour of television a child watches between the ages of one and three, the child had a nearly 10 percent higher chance of receiving an ADHD diagnosis by age seven. Toddlers in the study who watched three or more hours of infant television daily had a nearly 30 percent higher chance of having attention problems in school. We can combine this with the already existing knowledge that the average American household has the television on for about seven hours per day, watching on average 1,023 hours of television per year, and that 26 percent of American children younger than two have a television in their bedrooms. Many even watch television from their crib. According to the Kaiser Family Foundation, 36 percent of families leave the television set on almost all the time, even when no one is watching it. The average eighteen-year-old in the United States will have spent twenty-two thousand hours watching television.

The experience of teachers in the classroom can also support the observation that with the increase of electronic media, today's children are having more and more difficulty focusing in school. In my morning class recently, I asked a group of twenty-three eighth grade children to read a story by Jack London. "To Build a Fire" tends to be one of the more high-interest stories taught in middle school; it is read throughout the country by students and has been enjoyed for generations. I instructed the students that they would all be called upon to read a paragraph and that they were expected to follow along when it was not their turn to read. The "random call" technique is used by teachers to keep all students engaged, because no student knows when it will be his or her turn to read. I began the reading and then called Jennifer, a reliable girl in the front row, to take the second turn reading. The students seemed interested in the topic of the story, and I felt like I had them hooked before we even began with a discussion of life in Alaska, dogsleds and frozen limbs. But by the time the third reader had finished, half the class's attention was drifting away. I could see students drawing on their notebooks. Bobby, a boy in the back of the classroom, tried to sneak a comic book out from his desk and into his textbook; another boy in back of the room was doodling with marker on his arm; Michael, the child we spoke of earlier, was fidgeting, tapping his desk and squirming in his seat. I called on Chuck to read and, in response, got a confused look. "I don't know where we are," he said. I redirected the class, reiterated my instructions to follow along, please, and continued. But Kyle, the next reader, was lost, as was the next, and the next. I began to realize that even the most high-interest stories, and the most succinct of those, are not sufficient to sustain the attention of today's children who have been raised on warp speed visual imagery and the constant sensory bombardment of television and video games. Reading stories, even the most exciting on the market, as one boy put it, "are just too slow."

There are other factors at work as well, while the television set is on. The constant noise of the television may interfere with what is called inner speech. Inner speech is the internal dialogue children develop during the ages of two and three. Since many experiences, and the images that accompany them, are new to children of this age, their brains must support a process for making meaning of these new experiences. Jane Healy, a childhood brain expert who commented on the Christakis report in *Pediatrics*, says that children develop an internal dialogue whose domain is to think through problems, work out solutions and develop impulse control. During the time spent watching television, what she calls "mesmerization time," no development of the internal dialogue takes place, and thus this area of the brain becomes underdeveloped in children who watch too much television. What results are children who cannot control their impulses, who cannot think through problems to a rational solution and who need constant physical and mental stimulation to support their norms.

The Christakis study serves notice to parents and teachers that we may be making a terrible mistake by allowing our children unlimited access to television programs. I have taught classes where so many of the students in the room were squirming in their seats, unable to focus, unable to stop tapping their feet, clanking their pens or fidgeting that there was zero chance for anyone in the room to learn anything. Children with an ADD/ADHD diagnosis are almost always boys and frequently reject medical interventions because, they say, the drugs make them lose weight, feel sluggish or make them feel flat and unengaged. It is fair to say that ADD/ADHD and the impairments caused by television is a developing epidemic in America.

Of course, all of this begs the question, "How much television is too much television for a young child?" Recent research seems to indicate that some is bad, more is worse and none at all would be best. In Michael Gurian's *The Minds of Boys*, he cites a survey conducted by Dr. Barbara Brock of Eastern Washington University in which she convinced fifty fourth- and sixth-graders to "go without screens" for thirty days. No television. No computers. No video games. These were children who, in their lives before the study, had watched essentially the average amount of television and electronic media. Of the fifty children who began the study, only one-quarter of the participants "fell off the wagon" during the thirty days. The remaining three-quarters of the children showed improved grades, higher quality sleep, brighter moods and significant increases in family relationships. The time that was once spent in front of the television and computer monitor, Dr. Brock noted, was now spent in one of three activity domains: going outdoors, talking with family and friends or reading and game playing. We notice that the activities that take place with children when they are not in front of a screen are not at all passive, but instead active brain stimulations that develop language, creativity, communication and the foundations for vertical mindedness.

These studies show that, in general, all stimuli is not good for the developing brain and that electronic stimuli damages the developing brain and its ability to develop complex reasoning skills in the neocortex, the area where language, art, mythology, appreciation of one's environment and problem solving occur. The damage to children's ability to develop language is probably the most severe of all of these electronically-caused impairments. In addition, the time occupied by television is so significant that family relationships, friendships and overall emotional development are stunted.

Too many parents, reflecting the nation's overall acceptance of television as the primary cultural teacher of our children, have decided to allow television into their homes and in front of their children on a more and more widespread basis. As Lynette Clemetson reported in the *New York Times* in 2006, parents now feel that "the benefits of a little tube time—whether for their children's development or their own sanity—outweigh the risk of raising a generation of crib potatoes." We can hardly blame parents for this attitude. Americans are working harder than ever, are more tired than ever, and television, consequently, has become more normalized in the home than ever before. To say it is tempting to park the kids in front of the television while mom or dad enjoys a little downtime is a gross understatement. But the Kaiser Foundation report, on which Clemetson's article was based, shows this as being more than an occasional bit of relief that parents are seeking. 61 percent of babies under a year old watch television or videos on a daily basis, with an average viewing time of over an hour. One-third of the children under age six polled in the study had their own television set in their bedrooms. Their parents self-reported that the main reason for providing the television for their child's bedrooms was so that they could watch their own shows. Vicky Rideout of the Kaiser Foundation called parents' attitude towards television "enthusiastic" and television a source of parenting "assistance." It seems parents today are viewing the television set as almost another family member, a sort of electronic au pair.

Television programs aimed at young children have taken on a pervasive dimension in the past few years. Not only are there more programs aimed at children under age three, but also there are now entire networks, such as BabyFirst TV, that are marketed directly at toddlers. Their marketing message, which many parents seem to have bought into but is not backed by any sound research, is that the programming content is beneficial to children. It seems that parents ignore the pediatrician's advice to keep all television away from children under two as long as there is someone who claims it is acceptable, even if that someone stands to make a great deal of money from the transaction. Too often, I believe, we choose to believe what conveniently fits into our lifestyle.

The Teenage Media Conspiracy

It may not be going too far to say that some companies that control electronic media are conspiring to control the hearts, minds, brains, behaviors and, ultimately, the pocketbooks of teenagers. With thirty-two million members, this is the largest generation of American teenagers in our history and they have the most disposable income of any consumer group. Teens spend more than one hundred billion dollars a year on themselves and have at least some control of another fifty billion their parents spend on them. The competition for these dollars, as one can expect, is extremely fierce and the moral oversight of those competing for the teen market is virtually nonexistent.

Six major companies control virtually all of the television, music, movies and other lifestyle choices that teenagers see, hear, touch and feel: Newscorp, Disney, Viacom, NBC Universal, AOL/Time Warner and Sony. Their portfolios control upwards of 90 percent of the television, music, movies, internet, clothing, books, magazines, sports teams, cable networks, theme parks and video games teenagers consume. The Big Six's grip on teen life is so extensive, so massive, that their annual revenues (close to two hundred billion in 2005) rival the gross domestic product of many industrialized nations. Together, the Big Six have tremendous influence over American children. For example, the typical

American teenager will see and process an estimated two thousand advertisements from the Big Six each day and will see close to ten million of their ads by the time they turn eighteen, reports PBS's *Frontline: The Merchants of Cool.*

One of the tactics advertisers who target teenagers use is the strategy known as "lifestyle implanting." Marketers look for ways to insert not only their products, but also the demand for their products into teen culture. They accomplish this by selling not only soft drinks and sneakers, but also lifestyle images. Hip-hop culture, for example, was partly manufactured by clothing producers and music conglomerates who recognized a large untapped market in teenagers who were searching for a way to emulate the urban culture that was drifting out of Los Angeles and New York City in the 1980s. Similarly, marketers created the archetype of the prematurely sexual teenage girl in the late 1990s who flaunted her body yet controlled her destiny. Such pop performers as Britney Spears, Beyonce Knowles and Christina Aguilera exemplified this model, and soon teenage girls all over the country were emulating their brashness, buying their records, spraying their perfumes and wearing their branded clothing.

The Big Six and other companies that target teenagers employ what they call "culture spies" to investigate the latest trends in the teen world. They hire young people to interview other youths, pose in chat rooms and attend teen events in order to help identify cutting edge trends. In turn, they respond to those trends by developing products and marketing campaigns that tie into teens' needs and desires. Teen marketing companies may have more sociological data on teenagers than many of the top academic researchers in the nation.

Recently, marketers have developed a lifestyle model for teenage boys that fits very neatly with boys' testosterone-driven aggression and their adolescent anger and disaffectedness. Professional wrestling has become the single most popular form of entertainment for teenage boys and takes in more revenue than music, videos and movies. Live wrestling shows, pay-per-view events, product co-branding and cross-marketing platforms have given the Big Six and other companies billions of dollars of added revenue in the past few years. The WWE (World Wrestling Entertainment), the wrestling world's largest grossing company, aside from their live wrestling events, sells every product imaginable, from posters to computer wallpaper with pictures of muscle-bound wrestlers and their surgically enhanced female companions as well as cell phone ringtones. They were on track to take in a gross revenue of over 400 million dollars in 2006. But the lifestyle message that goes along with professional wrestling, video games and many professional sports not only advocates violence, but also places the uneducated, uninitiated, fatherless young man in the spotlight. The wrestling personalities that the WWE markets are turbocharged aggression wrapped in a tanned, muscular package. The images tell teenage boys that to be handsome, successful, powerful and popular with women, they must also be overtly brutal and aggressive. Curiously, the WWE has also recognized the yearn for fathers in today's boys. Their stable of performers boasts no less than five father-son wrestling duos who beat up on other pairs during their events. Teenage boys see in these aggressive, overly brutal warriors not a mythical hero, but a role model who teaches them that violent aggression pays. It is the same tactical message coming from video games, movies, television and other sources of teen culture. It is no wonder the recent generations of teenage boys have the attitudes they do regarding violence, competitiveness and aggression. It is as though the consumer marketplace has finally understood the chemical messages young men feel and has decided to capitalize on the worst aspects of those impulses in order to maximize revenue.

We have learned that the amount of exposure to a communication message determines how likely a person will be persuaded by that message. People who see a certain advertising message over and over again will be more likely to buy the product; people who hear the political candidate's message over and over again will be more likely to vote for that candidate and his or her ideas. As American professor and media critic Neil Postman argued in the 1980s, the prevalence of mass media has provided a forum for all types of unsophisticated and dangerous communication to affect those who pay attention to it. In the paternal age, communication media was accessed mainly by the initiated males—scholars, authors, elders—who had something meaningful to convey. As technology has improved, access to communication channels has become available to more and more people in society. Some have argued that open access to media was, and is, a good thing. Anyone today can simply log on to their favorite chat room and type in their ideas for all to see, and on-demand publishing has opened the world of books to just about anyone with a manuscript. But the danger we are experiencing with this continuing communications revolution is that all sorts of dangerous, unsophisticated and downright harmful messages are reaching children's ears without filters. As Postman maintained, kids are being taught the wrong things, in the wrong ways, by the wrong people. Those who dominate the media outlets popular with teenagers are not educators, elders or society's leaders; they are the marketers of clothing, books, music, movies, video games and other lifestyle products. Their motive is economic, and the side effects of their strategy are neither regulated nor filtered in any meaningful way.

Shedding

Another factor impacting how culture affects brain evolution is the process by which the developing brain sheds and gains synaptic structure in the new brain. In 1983, French neurobiologist Jean-Pierre Changeux published a book called *L'Homme Neuronal* (The Neuronal Man) in which he establishes an account of what he calls the "Darwinism of the synapses." Changeux contends that the development of the brain undergoes an evolutionary-type "survival of the fittest neurons" from birth until puberty in response to cultural influences such as music, conversation, television and other socially unique factors. Changeux's theory is that there occurs constant pruning of the synapses; some die off, or are killed, in order to make way for more dominant or even more recent blooms that are stimulated by environmental factors. For example, according to this theory, if someone attends classes in a foreign language or develops a passion for the symphony, the brain will react to this stimulus by killing off some of the synapses that control something else, perhaps a former pursuit like word search puzzles, and develop new synaptic connections in their place. Changeux theorized the brain's adaptive changes worked on a Darwinian model where it could recognize redundancy, or areas in the brain that were no longer vital or being used, and thus could be shed in order to allow a new neural bloom or wave of growth to take place. Later research on rats supported these theories by identifying a 20 percent growth in brain neuron density in rats that were placed in a culturally rich and challenging environment. The rat experiments, however, added the important knowledge that the limitations of the brain's neural growth are not necessarily finite. That is, the brain does not automatically need to shed one level of understanding in order to permit another to develop.

These theories constitute a basis for reasoning that an artistically rich culture will help the brain expand and develop; and if this is so, we must assume the reverse as well: that a culturally deprived environment will contribute to diminished development in the brain. We should combine this in the context of knowledge which argues that the brain's evolutionary development is both occurring in real time, in response to real environmental changes, and throughout time, genetically, generation upon generation, as all facets of our species' physical evolution have always occurred. We can then say that living in a diminished cultural environment, where television, computers, video games and lower forms of communication have since taken the upper hand, has resulted in a diminished level of brain evolution or, in a worst case scenario, as Pearce's book title suggests, we have reached *Evolution's End*, at least in terms of brain evolution.

TV and Language Development

But in Huxley's vision, no Big Brother is required to deprive people of their autonomy, maturity and history. As he saw it, people will come to love their oppression, to adore the technologies that undo their capacities to think.

Neil Postman, *Amusing Ourselves to Death*

Increasingly in the horizontal society, boys, in fact, most children of both sexes, learn to speak and think from watching copious amounts of television during the critical developmental periods in their lives. Researchers have developed a theory about language acquisition in children that is important to our discussion. They believe that children who grow up in a language-poor environment fail to develop the physical structures in the brain that enable us as adults to interpret complex language. Television does precisely the opposite of what the developing brain needs: it supplies an overload of sensory stimulation that negates the development of the language structures in the brain. If we examine this possibility closely, we can see that the implications for society are immense.

Language authorities contend that the notion of language is both genetically hardwired and developed in response to environmental conditions in humans. That is to say, it did not develop as a response to environmental influences alone, but was part of what we might call a cognitive coalition consisting of the very primal makeup of humanity as well as some inner need for our kind to communicate. The human brain is hardwired with a yearning to rise up, and written and verbal language is the mechanism it uses in that endeavor. But in coalition with the genetic component, environmental responses are equally important. So we see in the brain's language area much what scientists are finding in the brain as a whole: it has its independent parts—the neocortex, the brain stem and the limbic system, for example, all of which have their own component functions. But none of these areas is able to work in isolation, and all correspond to create a holistic brain function. None can act by itself. Along the same lines of logic, the brain's language areas develop mostly independent modules of function that find themselves working together: synaptic webs of interconnected pathways. But the genetic equation the brain uses to develop these connections is nurtured by environmental influences, such as verbal talk time with adults, reading, being read to, communicating in above level language conversations and listening to live, complex language and its associated meanings. However, as much as the positive effects of these language activities are known, information is now being discovered about the negative impacts of electronic media on boys' brain development as it relates to language acquisition. What we are seeing in the horizontal society is that the positive forces of literacy and language are subsiding and the negative forces of electronic media are increasing—a trend identified over twenty years ago and now omnipotent in our culture.

Scientists know that even in utero, a seven-month-old fetus responds to language heard from outside the womb, primarily that of the mother. They have been able to measure muscular responses in the fetus when the mother speaks. Moreover, the brain develops synaptic linkages that allow for language understanding during early childhood—between the ages of about three and seven and, some contend, even earlier, in the womb as a fetus. The linkages in the brain that allow for language learning are called ganglia, and they are physical structures, much like an interconnected braid of telephone wire; the more cable that is spun in the language part of the brain during these brief developmental windows, and the more finely woven it is, the more language a child will be capable of learning and understanding, both immediately and later in life. This is because these language pathways only have a short developmental window when conditions permit them to thrive, and once developed, or underdeveloped, major adjustments are not forthcoming. If the highways in the brain that carry language never fully develop, the child can have immense amounts of educational interventions and never be able to construct meaning from language to any significant degree. Think of it like building a highway system like the 495 beltway around Washington, D.C. Without the wide lanes and bridges, traffic would be at a complete standstill. The same holds true inside the child's brain: the construction season for neural pathways in the brain is very short, and without the right kind of work during those periods there will never be an efficient route for language traffic. As a result, I have seen in American classrooms a whole generation of boys who missed the opportunity to develop the capacity for complex reading, writing and communications.

The ability to use language to pair names with things and respond to emotions verbally is the hallmark of language development in young children. Many parents know that the first words spoken by their babies are not mere repetitions, but emotional responses. Statements like "No!" from a baby's lips are signs that the child is developing the synaptic connection between the thing (the emotion of frustration, for example) and the linguistic representation of it. They convey much of their language knowledge with tone, since their vocabularies and other language tools are not yet fully developed. One of the highest developments of the language category is the intrusion of the abstract into the child's world. This may be the child's first foray into vertical thinking, and it likely comes much easier to small children than adults who have been trained to shed both the rational dealings with abstract matters and the physical structures in the brain that deal with them. Many children begin speaking of a mysterious "other" at a very young age, perhaps an imaginary friend who comes to visit, even carrying on conversations with toys and animals that are imagined to be all manner of abstract relationships. Hearing a child carry on an imaginary conversation shows, I feel from watching my own child, the brain's language system working and developing. The imagination of the child is immense in its developmental spurts, and this is a credit to language development taking place at very high levels.

The emotional attachment to language in children also has a physical element. At the earliest ages, children learn names for things from parents or other adults in their household. The toddler may look at the refrigerator and point excitedly. It is clear to the parent that the child is searching for a name for the object, and he or she is compelled to assist. "That's the refrigerator, Sammie!" the parent may say excitedly. But it is not just the word given to the item that is learned by the toddler. The next time the child attempts to use the word again for identification purposes, he will place with it the emotional context of the word that was present when he or she learned it. "Refrigerator" will be a source of excitement—the object he or she wants is in there! The opposite is also true. The child is now three or four and is preparing to go to pre-kinder-garten. Mother was not fond of school, and she explains to her child that, "You're going to *school* tomorrow," in a tone of resignation or anger. The child will embed that negative emotion as well. Even though he does not fully understand the meaning, the child understands the negativity now assigned to the word. These emotional connections link together with the linguistic meaning in the synaptic development of the brain's language center. Emotional highways are spun the same as language highways. In fact, the two may be separate lanes on the same road.

The synaptic structures in the brain that promote language grow like weeds with wild energy when presented with the right conditions at the right time. That is to say, they behave as a growth spurt in the adolescent's body does, at a certain time in response to certain stimuli. But unlike the physical growth in the adolescent body, which can continue until age twenty, the physical changes in the brain happen at a much younger age and have a narrower window of opportunity to grow. Moreover, unlike the overall growth in the body, drugs, such as human growth hormone, cannot influence the rate of synaptic growth, nor can other artificial interventions. The brain's language centers develop in response to "organic" language stimulation that is heard, seen and experienced in the child's environment—primarily their home.

I mean to make a distinction here, as well, between home and school, because it is in the home around the parent or caregiver where the lion's share of language acquisition occurs, not in the classroom, as is sometimes believed. By the time a boy enters public school, at about age five or slightly earlier in pre-kindergarten programs, most of the language highways in the brain have already been built and the construction crews have moved on. Once the developmental window is closed, there is really no going back, at least in any meaningful sense. Most schools put a strong emphasis on remediation over early intervention, and state and federal education law encourages this as well. They take eight-, ten- or fifteen-year-olds who are judged to be "below ability level" and attempt to bring them up to speed academically. States such as New York even have mandatory interventions for students who do not score well on language tests. The problem with this strategy is that remediation is ineffective if the child's brain has not developed the capacity to learn the material in a meaningful way. However, there is a shift in understanding taking place in the schools; most teachers understand from experience that by the time these students are tested and shown to be below level in language, it may be far too late to do much about it. Early intervention with the preschool population is much more effective. However, the school often does not attain its authority over children until it is mainly too late, and American parents, for understandable reasons, have never been very enamored with the idea of letting someone else teach their preschoolers.

To understand how a child's brain develops the ability to learn and comprehend language requires a portion of anatomy and physiology. Researchers have been able to do quite a bit of brain mapping in recent years. They have been able to distinguish much of the specific areas of the brain that control major physical, emotional and social functions. For our purposes we can think of the brain as evolving in three distinct layers, or what the father of this line of thinking, neuroscientist Paul D. MacLean, called the "triune system." The inner layer can be called the "hind" brain or the reptilian brain (R-brain), which includes the brain stem and the areas that control basic physical functions such as breathing. Some have called this part of the brain the "executive office," because it maintains a certain authority over the other two parts of the brain. The R-brain is responsible for survival: the fight or flight reactions that may make the difference between an ancient warrior being pierced through the heart with a wooden spear or an ancient hunter on the steppes being stabbed by a mastodon's tusk. The R-brain is the oldest portion and was evolution's first attempt at humanity. As such, it maintains not only a substantial influence over the brain's overall functions, but a more essential, hub-like profile in the brain. It warrants executive authority over other functions. This part of the brain is the one that predates the modern era. It is responsible for reflexive learning and action; for example, the understanding that if one touches fire one will experience pain. It gives us the impulse to run away when danger lurks. Conditioned learning and simple emotional responses such as anger, hostility and anxiety dwell in the R-brain, as do the sexual drive, hunger and other core survival functions. Some, such as American professor and neuro-surgeon Karl Pribram, suggest that we call this part of the brain the "core brain," because it controls that which is at the core of our survival.

Evolution, for the most part, is a slow process, but culture changes quickly. One of the characteristics of brain evolution is that functions and capacities that develop remain in place even after their usefulness has subsided, which becomes especially apparent if fast-moving environmental changes intercede. Some now believe that a number of the survival functions the R-brain developed long ago are no longer necessary. For example, we no longer need to face-off against a mastodon or fight one another over the last scraps of food. However, the ease of modern life may have left us with R-brain instincts that have nowhere to go and are thus being channeled into other areas of our life and culture. One might say that the violence and "warrior" attitude that is present in many teenage boys may be the R-brain's instincts prevailing.

The middle layer of the brain is responsible for the feeling portion of our understanding and is sometimes called the limbic system

(MacLean's term). This part of the brain is most closely associated with the old R-brain, was the second section of the human brain to develop, and is responsible for processing incoming stimuli. It is what makes us respond negatively to the smell of sewage and react with the proper emotion when we stumble upon a snake in our path. It stores data about previous positive and negative experiences and assigns reactions to new experiences that may be related to the data available from previous experiences. The limbic system also controls the immune system, parent-child bonding, the complex feelings and emotions associated with relationships and the subtle intuitive systems related to dreaming and the subconscious. It is the mechanism that creates a man's love for a woman, the deep appreciation of a child, the core personal virtues that make up the individual. The limbic system also serves to connect the old R-brain to the upper level activities in the neocortex, or new brain, so that all three units can function as a whole.

The outer layer of the brain, the one that handles higher-level thinking and the one that is most in play in the electronic age, developed after the R-brain had established itself and the limbic layer had added upon that. The new brain, where the neocortex resides, for perspective, is five times larger than the R-brain and the limbic brain areas combined, yet has only been around for a fraction of a second of evolutionary time. Think of it this way: If you were to look at a cartoon showing the evolutionary development of the human brain, it would first appear as a small rod of fleshy matter bent over like a horseshoe. As time progresses and the limbic system develops, another thin layer is added, so that the structure now seems to resemble an onion or an avocado, with a dense core and an obviously different, newer layer of matter over it. Finally, the prefrontal lobes develop: the ball is covered with another layer, one built atop the first ball and the limbic layer that remain at the center. The new layer soon subdivides and develops specific areas for handling problem solving, complex emotion and, especially, complicated language understanding. Higher-level learning occurs in the prefrontal lobes in the new brain. Since evolution is an ongoing process, the natural area for new development and changes to the existing structure is the new brain. Brain evolution has, at least at first glance, not ended, but just begun, if we are to take the optimist's perspective. We know that evolution is ongoing, that monumental changes have already taken place, and with the expansion of knowledge and communication in the modern era, we might think that this is the very dawn of human brain development. There is another school of thought as well, one not quite so optimistic. The pessimists believe that we may in fact be entering the final stages of human brain evolution, slipping down a steep slope of our own creation into a deep, horizontal pit where the brain can no longer rise up.

When people say that we are only using a small portion of our brain, they really mean that the R-brain is occupied with the necessary physical processes of life and the prefrontal lobes, the learning brain, is only a bridesmaid waiting for a phone call from her boyfriend to begin the relationship. The bottom line for our purposes is that any real intellectual activity of a complex nature only happens in the new brain—the prefrontal lobes and the neocortex—but cannot happen without a coalition with the limbic system and the R-brain, for all brain functions are to some extent interconnected. The development of the neocortex is so new that from an evolutionary perspective it has not yet begun to fulfill its potential. To use Brower's clock metaphor, if the history of brain development were a twenty-four hour day, the neocortex may only have been around for twenty minutes or so, and there may be another twenty-three or so hours of development still ahead of us.

Most of the learning that takes place in schools today is not really learning that the new brain can sink its metaphorical teeth into, but rather conditioning that only stimulates the reptilian part of the brain, and to some extent the limbic system, as well as some very specific pragmatic functions in the new brain, which are now responding by becoming dominant. Children memorize seating assignments, their class schedules, the rules for a fire drill, over and over again. The same kind of repetitive conditioning takes place in math and language classes as well as other subjects. In the younger grades, children memorize the multiplication table, verbs and nouns, phonics cues and facts such as one must read left to right and top to bottom on a page of text. At the higher grade levels, students undertake the same kind of learning. In high school, they might memorize SAT vocabulary lists in the morning and the periodic table of elements in the afternoon. In the education world, this type of conditioning is called *rote learning*, but it is not really learning at all, it is memorization and conditioning. Rote learning takes place almost exclusively in the R-brain and limbic system. Therefore, we can think of it as a lower form of learning. This type of learning is also the foundation of most scientific arenas, or study based upon already founded and accepted premises. American schoolchildren learn in what I call "horizontal workshops" that only focus on pragmatic, or application-oriented, activities.

One of the greatest things about the triune brain, or "trimodal brain" as some have called it, is that the three seemingly independent systems have learned to co-exist and work together in most human functions. Their unity is what makes humans special and different from other animals. For example, even basic functions like excretion take on trimodal collaboration in humans. The urge to excrete comes from the R-brain, which sends a message through the limbic system, which in turn recalls previous experiences and connects an emotional element to the problem. "Should I use the upstairs bathroom or the downstairs so as not to disturb my wife?" the limbic system asks. The complicated contingencies are thus addressed and weighted by the new brain, the decision maker, using all available information that is passed along through the two animal brains, until it can come to a logical solution most likely to result in success. One might compare the differences between the brains of apes and humans in the context of the three-brain model. The R-brain handles the urges and needs necessary for survival, such as what occurs in the ape pen at the zoo when a meal is tossed into the cage housing the mother and child chimpanzee. However, without the triune brain system, it is simply a race for a meal. Humans take the relationship further and add deeper meaning;

such instances may become as complicated as Hamlet's or Oedipus' stories, due to the emotional connectivity afforded by the new brain.

The problem we face today is that learning is focused mainly on the pragmatic parts of the brain, not the intuitive functions, and without a blend of the two we cannot achieve our potential. We should never think of the R-brain, or its two upper neighbors, as working independently. We can see this clearly in the area of language. We know the R-brain is involved in language to some extent because of the measurable response fetuses have to language in the womb. But we also know that fetuses, or even one-year-olds, cannot master language until much later and after much more upper brain development has taken place. Therefore, you should not be misled when I say that the "language center" of the brain is solely in the new brain. Without the R-brain we would not have the motor skills to write; without the limbic system we would not have the emotional connections to the words, and so forth. Here, once again, we have to combine scientific thought with artistic concepts driven by anecdote and intuition to understand that the human brain is simultaneously three separate parts and one interconnected unit. The novelist F. Scott Fitzgerald once wrote, "The test of a first-rate intelligence is the ability to hold two opposed ideas in the mind at the same time, and still retain the ability to function."

It is at this point impossible to say to what extent we use our brains. We often hear the comment that, "Humans only use about 10 percent of their brain power." But this is unfounded and there is little in the way of research to prove it. We may be just as likely using only 1/100 of our brain's capacity, or 1/1000. We know that occasionally incredible feats of intellect or unattributable wisdom are shown to us, sometimes even demonstrated by our own minds. Some people do miraculous things and think miraculous things. We see these "miracles" performed by children as well as adults, so we know the human brain is capable of so much that we do not presently understand.

We just don't know the potential of the three brains or their combination. But we do know that the three-brain model is not the only system that works in humans. For example, there have been many reported cases of individuals whose neocortex was destroyed or never properly developed due to disease, such as those Roger Lewin examines in his article "Is Your Brain Really Necessary?" based on Professor John Lorber's research. Many of these people lived as fully functional adults, some even earning advanced degrees. It could be that in these cases, people were able to add capacity to their limbic and R-brains or that some areas took up the slack for the missing regions of the brain. It could also be that these compromised individuals fully developed the portion of the new brain that remained while most healthy adults only develop a small portion of it. There are many possibilities. In contrast, we do know that if certain areas of the brain are damaged, as is evidenced in thousands of stroke cases each year, other parts of the brain do not take over all the functions of the damaged parts and certain functions are lost forever. The human brain and its evolutionary development is a dynamic system.

Modern education rarely addresses more than one part of the brain's capacity and it treats the brain as though it were a static system. Conditioned learning does not stimulate neural brain growth during the developmental window in young children, mainly because it is focused in the R-brain (not to mention that most formal schooling begins after the important developmental windows have closed). Television and computer interaction is rote learning that does not stimulate brain development and may actually retard it. Pearce and other researchers have written about this phenomenon extensively, and it is becoming well documented. When children watch too much television, play too many video games, listen to too much background television noise or are exposed to too much radiant light from electronic sources, the developing brain suppresses the neural centers that control language and imagination—the front brain that is the last to develop and the easiest part of the brain to manipulate during childhood development. The latest research shows that it is not, as was once thought, the quality of the content that determines the effects of television on the brain, but the technology itself and the amount of time we are exposed to it as kids.

Children's brains (and adult brains to a lesser extent) have a predicable reaction to radiant light. Most of us have laid on the couch at one time or another and vegetated in front of the television set. We may have even thought at the time: *Boy, I have a lot to do but...I can always get to it later...I'm so comfortable right now.* Like the effect of the Lotus plant on Odysseus' men in the Greek epic *The Odyssey*, we are made catatonic by watching television. This, says Pearce, likely stems from the radiant light source that televisions and computer monitors use to display their images and reflective light, which develops the visual experience. Like other stimuli, the brain has a certain reaction to these sources of light. The brain goes into what we might call a "neutral" position, where higher level thinking does not take place and creativity, the center of imagination and language where imagery and art are interpreted, is turned off. This is why we may go into the television room and see our children sitting there as though hypnotized for hours on end. It is why seeing a Da Vinci painting on television is not the same experience as seeing the painting on the wall in a gallery.

However, in the child's developing brain, the effects of television are far worse than in the adult brain and may be permanent. Television's effect on the brains of children ages one to eleven go beyond the neutralizing state seen in adults. Children's brains may actually change physiologically and genetically from watching television. For example, the brain, the heart and other parts of the endocrine system release hormones whenever the body experiences something it perceives as an emergency. Again, it is the so-called fight-or-flight response the body and brain have developed over thousands of years in order to protect us when confronted with danger. Children's television programming and video games aimed at young adults contain purposeful "startle effects" that are meant to trigger this type of emergency reaction from the endocrine system. Television does this, contends Joseph Chilton Pearce in a *Journal of Family Life* interview, with both programming content, such as chases, fights, shootings and beatings, and cliffhangers as well as with "sudden and dramatic changes in light intensity...sound, and rapid-shifting camera angles." The television industry learned that as children watch more and more of this type of programming, and because of the increased popularity of high-action video games, kids are actually becoming habituated to the brain's reaction to this type of electronic stimuli. Like a drug addict who needs constantly increasing dosages to achieve the same effect, children are becoming numb to the impact of startle effects in their programs. The television industry is responding to this threat to their popularity by making their startle effects bolder, louder and more frequent in cartoons and other children's programs. Their main startle effect has become violence. Thus we are now seeing a generation of adolescents who are by most measures immune to the emotional effects of violence, who cannot feel complex remorse or empathy, and who now have brains conditioned to see violence as a means of communication.

Media researchers have studied thousands of hours of children's cartoons in the United States, Great Britain and Germany. What they have found is that on average there are sixteen individual acts of violence in every half-hour of children's cartoons aired on television. Watch any television program with your child and you will see characters beating one another with clubs, pushing each other off cliffs and occasionally using weaponry such as tanks, guns, knives and bombs. When children view such startle effects, their brain chemistry reacts by turning down the volume in the neocortex—the new brain—where rational emotion, problem solving and complex interpretation takes place; moreover, Pearce continues in the interview, the R-brain "sends a series of alarm messages upward to the emotional brain." These signals are carried by hormonal messengers, such as the powerful hormone cortisol. When the brain receives a blast of cortisol, immediately hundreds and thousands of neural links are formed in the R-brain, in preparation for fight or flight. The neocortex shuts down and goes into neutral mode. At the same time, the heart speeds up, the adrenal glands begin pumping and the body's chemistry changes.

In the United States, there has been a massive increase in the diagnosis of what has come to be called Chronic Fatigue Syndrome

(CFS), also known as Adrenal Fatigue, in adults ages twenty to forty. CFS essentially is when the adrenal glands stop working due to overuse. The adrenal glands, aside from being important to the fight-or-flight response, help regulate energy levels. When they stop working or under-produce, the effects are debilitating. Some researchers are now looking into the possibility that the rise in CFS in younger and middle-aged adults may come from too much exposure to television as children, too much activation of their fight-or-flight response.

Part of the problem with children's television is that it has become a constant barrage of startle effects. The average American boy has watched over five thousand hours of television by age six. This massive exposure to startle effects and the endocrine processes that come with it are causing genetic changes in the brain. Scientists have begun to call this phenomenon "brain regression" and "devolution." Psychological researchers in Germany have completed a long-term study of kids who have watched the average amount of television viewed by American children and who have completed their childhood brain development phase. The researchers have discovered severe neuro-cognitive diminishments in simple areas such as the ability to distinguish colors. The children in the test group lost over two-thirds of their ability to differentiate color gradients. More importantly, they discovered that the brains of these children were losing the ability to cross-index information. Cross-indexing is when the upper brain must draw on more than one piece of knowledge to solve a problem. For example, when looking at a three-dimensional diagram, subjects must determine both spatial relationships and written information to solve a problem. These are the types of relationships that the brains of television watchers are unable to comprehend.

Other researchers report that the devolutionary effects of television also affect the emotional areas of the brain. For example, when test subjects who had become used to watching television were placed in a neutral environment without excess visual stimulation, they became anxious, bored and more prone to violence. These same subjects also experienced a 20 percent reduction in their awareness of their natural environment. That is to say, they were no longer able to appreciate their surroundings (the very essence of mythological practice, we might recall, is to determine man's relationship with his environment). Therefore, we can say that watching too much television might be making us unaware of our environment, less appreciative of our natural surroundings, and complacent about our impact on them. Few would argue that humans in general have had a diminished appreciation for their environment in the television age. If we placed a graph of environmental damage next to a graph of television usage, I'm confident we'd see a correspondence.

Researchers at Purdue University's Infant Language Laboratory, led by George Hollich, recently completed a study showing that even the moderate background noise of a television in the household can affect a child's ability to learn language. Part of the problem with background noise, says Hollich, is that oral language does not have punctuation to provide context. Having more than one source of language in their environment prevents the child from concentrating on the real person speaking and thus diminishes meaning. Children need to look at the speaker's face and watch their lips move as well as hear their words clearly to develop language understanding. Hollich worked with seven-month-olds in his study by showing them a video of a person talking and emphasizing a specific word, such as "cup." While the person spoke in the video, another man spoke in the background about an unrelated subject. The children who learned from the video with the distracter noises showed delayed language learning. The researchers at Purdue found that children who learned in an environment where there were auditory distractions were developmentally delayed in an appreciable way in terms of their ability to learn new language. "The second and third experiments show that a second source of sound can interfere...and now we know being able to see something along with the audio in a noisy situation plays an important part in infants' language development," said Hollich.

The studies of ADHD and language acquisition show that television both diminishes the development of language centers in a child's brain and affects the brain's ability to process information at rapid speeds. We spoke earlier of the developing brain by using the metaphor of cell-phone transmitters or telegraph lines talking to one another through linkages in the neurons and synapses. But perhaps a better metaphor would be to think of the communication system in the brain as insulated electrical wires. The transmission wires are called axons; they carry electrical impulses and are wrapped, or sheathed, in myelin, an insulator that is composed mainly of fat. That is, the axons that really work at functional speeds are insulated in myelin, but not all axons have this important sheathing. Somehow, during the developmental phases, the brain knows which axon structures are being used purposefully, myelinates them for protection, and leaves the remainder for later shedding. The fatty insulation serves a purpose: it allows the electrical signals to travel much faster than in an unmyelinated axon— about one hundred times faster. The more insulated your axons, the more efficient your brain is at transmitting data, the more data it can transmit at one time, the more complex the data being processed can be. Interestingly, around age six, the foundational systems in the ancient structures of the R-brain and limbic system are largely complete, and the developmental focus turns to the newer structures of logic and reasoning in the neocortex. Myelination is a key element in this process.

One would think that the levels of insulation and the number and synchronicity of the axons and their adjoining structures are what separates, in a physical sense in the brain, adults from children. Newborns, for example, have very few myelinated axons. Therefore, their vision is diminutive, their motor coordination poor and their neurons reduce them to cooing when happy and crying when uncomfortable. One of the most important developmental stages takes place at about age eleven. It is during this developmental window that about 80 percent of the neural mass in the brain disappears. The brain releases chemical cleansers that adjoin to little used and unmyelinated neurons, wipes them away and leaves the child's brain with about the same net neural brain mass he had at eighteen months of age. Therefore, using and stimulating the right neuron and axon structures in the brain before age eleven, thus motivating myelination, is critical to which structures will survive the cleansing and be around for use for the rest of the child's life.

Researchers are now investigating the possibility that environmental influences, such as watching television, impact the myelination process and therefore affect the brain's language development in children. We know that certain language centers in the brain become myelinated just prior to a developmental window in children. For example, Broca's area, which is linked to language production, becomes myelinated just as children develop the ability to use speech and grammar—around age one. Wernicke's area, where language comprehension is centered, becomes myelinated several months before Broca's area. This is part of the brain's ingenious coordination, because language comprehension must develop prior to language production. If the two systems do not organize in that particular order during those particular developmental windows, the person's ability to learn language throughout his or her life will be impaired—forever. It is even more amazing to recognize that these developmental processes take place within only a few months, or even weeks, of one another, leaving little time, or room, for error.

Researchers believe that if a child does not receive the proper environmental stimulation, or receives detrimental environmental stimulation, during these crucial developmental windows, the complex organization of the neurons in these two language areas of the brain will not arrange properly. Moreover, it is also believed that the myelination process will either slow down or apply to the wrong areas at the wrong time if misdirected by disadvantageous stimuli. One theory is that exposure to electronic media during these crucial windows is specifically what causes retardation of the complicated and coordinated language processes in the child's brain.

One of the problems with brain research, of course, is that to truly understand what is happening inside the developing brain requires cutting open the skull and closely examining the microscopic structures contained therein as they develop. As you might guess, there are few parents willing to volunteer their children for such studies. But much progress has been made in recent years in our ability to see inside the brain without surgery. PET scans, particularly, have become amazingly clear and precise, but unfortunately still cannot see at the microscopic levels necessary for definitive evaluation. So once again we are confronted with the problem we've outlined: we know something is happening intuitively and inferentially—children's brain development is being subverted by watching television and watching other electronic media—but we can't quite prove it in detail scientifically. But much like a court case that has eyewitnesses, character witnesses, a criminal with a horrible record, an opportunity and a clear motive, we know the accused is guilty, but we don't yet have the DNA evidence necessary for a lopsided conviction. Thus the television set remains on.

Language Development

Terrible things can happen to children when their brains do not allow them to see mental pictures of the things they hear and read about. Without the ability to visualize the abstract and to think on a metaphoric level, little meaning can be extrapolated from human communication. Teacher Barbara Stanford described the language characteristics of America's children in the twenty-first century in a recent issue of *English Journal*:

> One day during my recent sabbatical, I was working
> with a small group of eighth-grade students who were reading
> aloud a passage in Ouida Sebestyen's Words by Heart. In
> the passage, the main character discovers her father's dead
> body. Students pronounced the words with little trouble. But
> when I asked them basic comprehension questions, most had
> no idea what happened.
>   "Who died in the passage?" I asked.
>   Most looked at me blankly. "Somebody died?"

*...Clearly they had read the words, but they had not
put the words together with a mental picture of the action.*

As Stanford noticed, and as I have noticed in my classroom, many of today's kids have the ability to read the words, but fewer of them are able to attach meaning to what they read, see and hear. The consequences of this are truly severe. If a child can read about a young girl discovering her father's dead body but not understand the meaning of loss or sorrow, how can they develop the proper empathic emotions that make them responsible humans? The answer is that they cannot. Since children are not connecting to the experiential and metaphoric aspect of the language, they are not developing empathy, sympathy, compassion or meaningful connections to nature, people and things. The violence and separateness that characterize today's youth culture is an understandable result of this basic disconnect.

The language stimulus that propels and supports growth in the language center of the child's brain comes from above-ability level conversation and other exposures to complex languages during the developmental windows, including verbal and imagistic language that is organic and not from an electronic source. That is to say, active engagement in language—conversations with adults and other children and reading and writing with those whose language capacity surpasses their own. It does not come from passive language learning, such as watching television, reading pages on the Internet or listening to music. As a teacher, I can vouch for the fact that children who come from homes whose inhabitants read, speak and write at a low language level will rarely surpass that language level in their own learning, regardless of the interventions at school. A common saying among educators when they meet parents who closely resemble their children is "the apple doesn't fall far from the tree." It is true in terms of language acquisition in children, because they do not engage in language activities at home with parents who don't value well-developed language skills.

Studies have shown that parents—specifically fathers—spend only about ten minutes per day talking to their children and even less time reading with them. Conversations, which have grown rare and sparse in the modern era, are what trigger the brain development in children that relates to language. All of us who have parented toddlers or recall our younger brothers and sisters know that children will learn something new, embed it as a routine and grow very attached to that "normal" pattern of interaction. Routines are important to children in order to make them feel comfortable and safe. However, when it comes to language, placing names to things and associating the corresponding emotional connotations to language, routine can be extremely detrimental. The comfort with repetition may be a developmental tension between the older and newer neuronic pathways in the brain. As the new brain continues to spin its growing web of language pathways in early childhood, the shedding of the older structures tends to rebel and scream out for safety. To be safe and survive, their host must not learn new language skills, and thus there builds an evolutionary conflict between the yearning for new knowledge and the comfort of passivity. How many children would themselves choose the discomfort of new learning over the safety and ease of passivity? Very few. Which is exactly why parents and other caregivers are essential to motivate the child and provide language stimulation from early childhood through adolescence.

To understand how children acquire language, one study took a group of children and gave them a fourth-grade-level text. The first group was given the text on paper; the second was shown the text on a movie screen; the third viewed it on a television screen. Less than a half hour later they were tested on their retention of the material. Those who held the paper copy in their hands retained 85 percent of the material. Those who saw it on a movie screen retained 25–30 percent. Those who viewed it on a television screen retained less than 5 percent. Language development clearly can only effectively be achieved through reading texts and participating in verbal dialogue, or what I call organic language.

What do we mean by language? There are many interpretations of this word. In early childhood, we mean language in a most literal sense. This is the time where kids develop the ability—and the physical structures in the brain—to use and manipulate words, expression, vocabulary and syntax. If the child is exposed to the right kind of language in the right contexts during these peek periods of development, they will then have the physical structures in the new brain to appreciate a beautiful poem, gaze inspiringly at a coastal sunset, write the great American novel or simply experience the world as a language-based organism. Interpretations of symbol, metaphor and image are the most complex type of language. The language attribute, acquired in early childhood, once established, develops into the artistic capacity in adolescents and adults. Without the language structures from early childhood, there can be no art, no higher-level thinking and no relationship with the world other than on a horizontal, literal level. Not having the early exposure to language prevents a child from ever again being able to experience the world on a figurative level. This is the immense consequence of language denial that I spoke of earlier.

Language is a code system. More particularly, it is a series of unique code systems, some debilitatingly complex, others so simple that they can be mastered in a matter of minutes by any four-year-old. But it is the type of code system we use with children at the proper time in their synaptic development that makes or breaks their brains' opportunity to reach higher, develop further and "go vertical" someday, as it were. Developing the ability to understand new code systems is a skill that can be applied to all subject areas, not just reading and writing. Higher math, physics, architecture, accounting, engineering, computer science, medicine and many other disciplines rely on language-based code systems. Try writing a computer program or calculating the angles in a girder system if you disagree.

For example, a moderately complex code system—for instance, English language vocabulary at the ninth or tenth grade level—can positively stupefy an American English language speaker in the ninth grade. I am constantly reminding myself when I speak with students to "turn down the vocabulary volume, or they'll have no idea what I'm talking about." My brain might be telling me to say to the class, "Your writing in this essay meandered between imperfection and outright nonsense." But I have to stop and tell myself to say, "Kids, these papers stink!" Otherwise they will have no idea what I mean.

This predicament is contrary to everything I learned about language in graduate school. Universities teach teachers that vocabulary should always be presented at a slightly higher level than the student is currently using, so that they may contact new words, expand their personal dictionaries and develop broader language code systems. But in my experience this is only true for younger children whose brains are still developing their language centers. The adolescents I work with, when confronted with new vocabulary, simply shut down and do not comprehend. Their brains seem to have lost the will or the ability to try and interpret new codes. Most disturbingly, the vocabulary level of most adolescents (and many adults) has dropped to its lowest point in decades.

This dumbing-down of the code system is multigenerational and has impacted the deepest part of the communal brain as well as the very purposeful evolutionary development of the language centers in the brain. This is no wonder when we take into account that the language children most often hear is coming from the television. Two out of five grade-school-age children currently come home to a house empty of adults. Moreover, if the adults are present, they are so tired, worn, busy or otherwise disengaged that their language time with their children is almost nonexistent.

The current disregard for language grammar and syntax is partly to blame for this disturbing trend. I have actually been reprimanded by school administrators for teaching grammar to my middle-school English classes. They felt the practice unworthy of class time. Grammar and syntax forces the brain to strive to make meaning out of complex symbols and develops the organizational skills necessary to communicate effectively. The greatest benefit is the ability to express and understand emotion verbally and syntactically. For example, a child may be feeling poorly. "I'm sad," the child explains to his parents. But there are a thousand causes and types of sadness. There may be an emotional problem in the child's life, an opportunity for the parent to teach about aggressiveness, friendship, sharing or communal knowledge. But these lessons will never develop when the child can only say, "I'm sad." It takes a properly formatted conversation to explain, "Jimmy stole my hat because I had teased him about his shirt the day before and Suzy, who Jimmy and I both like, thinks hats are attractive, and I may possibly lose my best friend due to petty jealousy and miscommunication." The study of complex vocabulary, grammar, syntactic structures, foreign languages and other code systems encourages the brain to grow and develop.

The opposition to reading is not only a characteristic of today's students, but also many of today's adults. One new teacher who was hired at a high school where I worked told me, "I don't much care for reading. Why read when there's so much cool stuff on television and movies?" The same resistance to reading is true of writing as well. Another teacher once stated proudly that she plagiarized her required Masters Thesis from the Internet. One college professor I know who works at a major university told me that he catches a plagiarized undergraduate paper at least once per semester. The language denial is present in the adult world, in the educational system and is growing exponentially among high school and college students. Some college professors tell me that when students come to them for their admissions counseling sessions and it comes time to declare a major, the students often ask, "What will require the least amount of writing?" Some college students are choosing their majors based upon how little language interaction they will need.

In December 2005, the National Center for Education Statistics released the results of a report called "A First Look at the Literacy of America's Adults in the 21st Century." Among other findings, the survey concluded that thirty million adults in America have below basic literacy skills, including seven million adults who are considered to be non-literate in English. Commenting on the findings in a *Washington Post* article by Lois Romano, the president of the American Library Association, Michael Gorman, said, "It's appalling—it's really astounding. Only 31 percent of college graduates can read a complex book and extrapolate information from it. That's not saying much for the remainder."

The tests that revealed the findings were not unduly rigorous. Nineteen thousand people were asked to read prose (informational documents such as two opposing editorial viewpoints) and answer some basic questions about the material. Of the college graduates in the survey, only 31 percent were classified as proficient, a decline of nearly 10 percent since the last survey in 1992. Our nation is trending towards illiteracy at an appalling rate. The survey results had only been out for a matter of hours when pundits began condemning the teachers and schools of America for the problem. Even ALA president Gorman condemned the schools. "There is a failure in the core values of education," Romano quoted Gorman as saying. But in the same article, Mark S. Schneider, commissioner of education statistics, hit the nail on the head when he said, "It may be that institutions have not yet figured out how to teach a whole generation of students who learned to read on the computer and who watch more T.V."

One recent study of children conducted by Dr. Bernia Collenci of New York University found that 90 percent of fifth graders in America read less than four minutes a day. Ten percent of them do not read at all. In the schools where I teach, it is not unusual to get a student at the high school level who is functionally illiterate. Early in my teaching career I took a job substitute teaching tenth grade English at a mid-sized public school. I was there for ten weeks covering the regular teacher's maternity leave. The first day of class, I wrote the objective for the class on the blackboard: *Students will learn the expectations and steps necessary for success in Mr. Carmichiel's English class.* After introducing myself, I called upon one of my male students in the class at random to read the objective out loud for the class. He flatly refused. I shrugged it off and asked another boy. He refused to read the objective as well. I was baffled. Did I walk into a school filled with oppositional adolescents?

Not wanting to cause a confrontation in front of my new class, I maneuvered around the predicament and read the objective myself, then continued teaching the rules and procedures that would be part of my classroom expectations. Later in the day, in the staff lunchroom, I told one of the special education teachers I had come to know about what had happened in class. "Oh, I should have warned you," she said. "Shawn, Danny, Carole and Brad, I think in that class, can't read at all. Try not to call on them." I had inherited a class of average tenth graders, fourteen- and fifteen-year-olds, none classified as learning disabled, in which at least four of twenty could not read a simple sentence.

Since that time, I have worked with many students who were non-readers at the high school level. Often these students receive remediation, sometimes including programs such as the Wilson Phonics Course, in addition to their regular classroom course load. Rarely, however, does reading remediation work once the student has reached a particular age. Some of these students do learn to read—and the Wilson program and other phonics programs are a testament to the potential to make readers out of adult non-readers—but the margins and abilities of those students who begin language learning in their teen years or older is miniscule compared to the younger age groups. When a child learns to read at a late age, both their reading and comprehension abilities are mechanical and lack connections to other meanings.

In almost all of the cases of students who come to me in high school who are functionally illiterate, I have found some striking similarities. Most of the non-readers are boys and most of the homes where these boys grew up did not contain books, reading material or any kind of language practice other than television. In fact, I can't think of a single high school non-reader whom I have worked with who grew up with storybooks or any type of reading material in the home when they were toddlers. However, in many of these cases, the parents or caregivers in the home could read and most had finished high school. These experiences started me thinking that we are moving towards a non-literate society and that the trend away from a language-based world has not only begun, but has become embedded, especially in boys.

⑤

Complex Language and Poetry

The communication initiation necessary for children to develop the ability to interpret and interact with complex language does not come from popular culture. Adult television, for example, uses vocabulary somewhere around the fifth grade level. Even the evening news dumbs down its communication so as not to insult or alienate any viewer and tells its tales of flood and war in short, monosyllabic bursts that challenge no part of the brain. These electronic sources—computers, video games, television, popular music—do not stimulate the brain's language centers. Worse, some people have suggested they actually numb the brain's language centers with their constant barrage of below-grade-level vocabulary, sound bites, sports scores, jingles and catch phrases. Most everyone of a certain generation remembers the "Where's the Beef?" commercial and the McDonald's jingle. Television can very successfully implant ideas and messages into viewers' minds. How many of the same generation remember a single poem from those same years?

Poetry is one type of vertical language training that urges the developing language centers in the brain to reach higher. The poet Susan Astor once wrote:

Above and under, over and below,
The limbless mammals
Stroke the sea.

Day bubbles upward through the dark,
Night settles down
And still they move;
Warmed by their own warm blood,
They meet and rub
In the ocean's vast room.

Who are these porpoises and whales,
Who, unencumbered, pulse and wallop
Over shells and tentacles,
Past skitters of slim fish,
Around the islands of our continents
Loving without lips,
Nursing without noise…?

We pile our cities up like blocks
And climb them, chattering,
While underneath
The vowel-voiced animals
Just swim
And arch their bodies into smiles.

Even with the burning numbness of the hamburger jingle echoing in our brains, many of us can see the figurative language in the poem. The poem makes some sort of connection between humans and the sea creatures. There's a message about sameness, a shared world, a common life. There's something there about the people living in the cities above the water and the original joy of the creatures that do not. That level of understanding, which in some cases may resonate so deeply that the reader may in fact see what English poet William Blake called "The end of a golden string" (the fulcrum point, or change agent, that gives a person the moment of epiphany where they can then change their life), gives the reader an experiential moment in the language. We can call this experiential moment of psychic understanding with language a vertical moment, where the psyche is provided the opportunity to rise up, instead of just drifting along aimlessly, horizontally, on a calm sea of headline news and hamburger jingles. This is the moment where language changes the world, instead of just reflecting it. These vertical moments are exit points out of our cave and into the open air where all of the world's great thinking and achievement has taken place. Vertical thinking allows the development of the brain to spring upward. Without time for vertical thinking in early childhood and adolescence, the brain will not develop the synaptic connections necessary for evolutionary advancement.

Poet Pablo Neruda wrote:

And that is why I speak and sing
and see and live for all men:
it is my duty to tell what you don't know
and what you do know I'll sing with you:
your eyes accompany my words

Here again we see the vertical thinking of the mind initiated in language. The poem shows that one man has a duty to all men; that there is a duty to humanity, to other living things, to culture and the earth. Words are the ropes that connect the living things in the culture and allow for mass change and achievement. Without the physical structures to accept the vertical way of thinking, the psychic truth that must be experienced on the level of language, there can be no cultural advancement, only horizontal movement, which is really no movement at all, but more like looking in a mirror reflecting the same economic, social, political and personal values the culture has had all along. Looking in a mirror, as we have done for perhaps two hundred years or more, is okay if you believe that the image in the mirror is acceptable. But I think that few, even the most optimistic thinkers of our time, would look at America in the mirror today and say, "What a perfect beauty! Let's not change a thing!" Global warming, rampant crime, drug abuse, fatherless children and the overall decline of the family all tell us that the face we see in the mirror needs some shaping or a total makeover.

I always share a poem with my students on the last day of school. I copy it, read it aloud and hand it to them near the end of class. I tell them at the beginning that I am going to give them a gift "and it is likely something you won't appreciate now, but you may hold onto it for some time, take it out some day in the future when you need it, and gain a benefit from it." I give them a copy of American poet William Stafford's "A Ritual to Read to Each Other":

If you don't know the kind of person I am
and I don't know the kind of person you are
a pattern others made may prevail in the
    world
and following the wrong god home we may miss
    our star.

For there is many a small betrayal in the mind,
a shrug that lets the fragile sequence break
sending with shouts the horrible errors of childhood
storming out to play through the broken dike.

And as elephants parade holding each
  elephant's tail,
but if one wanders the circus won't find the
  park,
I call it cruel and maybe the root of all cruelty
to know what occurs but not recognize the fact.

And so I appeal to a voice, to something
  shadowy,
a remote important region in all who talk:
though we could fool each other, we should
  consider—
lest the parade of our mutual life get lost in the
  dark.

For it is important that awake people be awake,
or a breaking line may encourage them back to
  sleep;
the signals we give—yes or no, or maybe—
should be clear: the darkness around us is deep.

There is, I feel, no way to explain interdependence on an experiential level without symbolic poems like this. The metaphor in the poem seems clear to me, even obvious. The elephants represent us— humans—and their walk holding one another's tails demonstrates that we humans need to live communally if we are going to survive and prosper. It is one of the clearest messages I have ever come across in modern poetry and Stafford is a very direct, uncomplicated poet. I have used this last-day ritual for several years now, and have given the poem to students ranging in every grade from sixth through twelfth. The reaction I get from the class as they are leaving the room for the summer is always the same. First, they are disappointed that the gift I built up earlier in the period is a poem and not something edible. But second, they are usually completely confused about the message in the poem. "What the hell do elephants going to the circus have to do with us?" they ask each other; or, "Have a good summer Mr. Carmichiel; keep daydreaming about them elephants!" Trying to use metaphors or symbolic stories with some American teenagers today is about as easy as communicating with them in Latin or Swahili.

There are many dangers in having a generation of children who are not able to experience complex language. As Plato remarked, written language was the starting point of human intelligence. Writing a thought down gives rise to criticism and two-way communication. It places the thought in a position where it can be examined deeply, debated, investigated, researched and scrutinized. It provides the opportunity for cultural response, opinion formation and structures to form around the ideas. Take politics as one example. If a problem exists in society, new laws may be proposed and discussed among possible stakeholders. If the idea passes the verbal challenge, it may become drafted, sent to the media and printed in newspapers for constituents to evaluate. This process gives those affected by the proposed law a chance to respond and present their arguments about the law's value or lack thereof. Without the written form, governments would tend to lean toward authoritarianism and individuality, as well as the communal good, would be sacrificed. Writing an idea down also provides for broader meaning by inviting context into its evaluation. The spoken word is a moment in time. The written word lasts and gives people the opportunity to evaluate it now and in the future. It allows for us to compare its merits to what has happened historically, not just what is happening at the time it is said. Anthropologists have always viewed ancient cultures with written language as being superior in many measurable ways. Most importantly, when cultures go about making important judgments, decisions that may prove to one day be their undoing, they must gather the intellectual resources at their disposal, judge their decision in context of past and present experience and forecast the impact of their decision into the future. Such complex reasoning does not happen without a reservoir of written language and, some would argue, is happening less and less often in modern America because we are moving away from a literate culture.

The Quest

If these are some of the consequences that result from a lack of language development in children, then what can promote language advancement? American mythology professor and author Joseph Campbell, among others, argued that the human mind developed with roots in imagery and mythology. Early humans, with their cave paintings and initiation rituals, had one fundamental premise in their belief system: no matter what *knowns* were present in their life, life itself was a mystery, an unknown. Moreover, the process of investigating the mystery *is* the meaning of life. Their cave paintings expressed this quest for meaning in the mysteries of life. If we examine the art of some of the early cave dwellers, in places varying from the Lascaux Cave in France, to the Australian outback, to early Native American dwellings such as the petroglyphs of Newspaper Rock in Utah, which date from about A.D. 900, we can see a pattern. All of these peoples drew sketches of animals that bore little or only casual resemblance to any creature that had lived on the earth, past or present. Some were otherworldly, with sharp points jutting in all directions from their heads. Some were half man, half beast, with the torso of a human and the body of a deer. At Newspaper Rock, there are what clearly seem to be humans riding atop four-legged animals, right next to a picture of a horned man-beast with human limbs and the antlers of a bull or deer. Clearly, the early human mind was concerned with making sense of conflicting forces in their world: the need to respect the animal, yet harvest it for food; the need to love other humans, yet destroy them in battle; the notion that the animals were imbued with powerful spirits, yet had to be killed and eaten. These conflicts had no answers, so gods were invented, shaman initiated, vision quests undertaken and so on. A spiritual relationship was formed to make the interaction between the human and non-human world psychically acceptable. In a hundred different ways, humans all along have striven to make sense of the inherent confusions of their world. The language of mythology has always been their tool for this process.

Do we still today seek to understand the conflicts in our world, either through ritualistic or mythological means? Clearly, the answer is no. We rely on pragmatism, a belief that the answers must be applicable, that the world exists in a stratified group of black and white hierarchies and that there are no longer mysteries to be addressed. We have gone to the moon, conquered the Amazon, mastered agriculture, medicine and engineering to our satisfaction or, at least, our quests for understanding are only undertaken if they may end up in an application. Even our leaders assert that they have figured out beyond a shadow of a doubt the mystery of God and thus the origins of the universe (some recent presidents have claimed to be "born-again Christians" with a definitive understanding of religion). Most recently, President George W. Bush promoted the instruction of *intelligent design* in public schools, an explanation that the universe was likely created by a higher power and that the theory of evolution could be discounted. I feel the lack of inquiry has cemented our pragmatic paradigm in this period in human history.

What happens when a society only uses exploration for practical and economic purposes? What is the result of believing that one knows all the answers? Such a belief system takes away the need to examine complex questions. Once the brain (and here I mean both the personal brain and the communal brain) has stopped wrestling with the big questions, psychic growth essentially ends. Having spent a considerable amount of time on college campuses, I can testify that many of today's students are not on campus to delve into philosophy or the arts or throw their lives behind a mythological quest for greater understanding. Many are there for economic reasons, in the law schools, business schools and engineering colleges where their goals are high-paying careers. These professions, however necessary and admirable, are dwellings where the pragmatic mind resides. Contract law has already been written and engineering diagrams have already been recorded and patented. Public accounting principles have been agreed upon. Even software developers work from what is now a long established language that bares no resemblance to what we know of as human language. New knowledge in these areas and others is built upon existing knowledge. It is as though our culture has chosen to build upon the knowns, disavowing the idea that anything in the post-industrial world can yet be unknown.

So then, if a child comes into a world where mythological and symbolic language has been abandoned, the child will not be exposed to the language environment necessary during the developmental window in early childhood when language structures in the brain are being formed. The results can be disastrous, because this means that the brain fails to develop the ability to interpret symbolic and mythological systems for making meaning of the world and the child may have a deficit in the language area that can never be overcome. The child's brain is so fantastically complex that even with all of the advanced scientific understanding, all of the MRIs, PET scans, brain research and field study that researchers have undertaken in recent decades, there are still millions of questions left unanswered about how a child's brain develops and works. We know, for example, that only four weeks into gestation the baby's brain develops something in the neighborhood of 500,000 new neurons every minute, yet we have little idea how outside influences may affect the development of these neurons. We know where in the adult brain language is stored and processed. But we also know that during a person's lifetime, or because of injury or disease, these areas can change. Language can even shift from one hemisphere of the brain to another. We have absolutely no idea why. The brain is a landscape that we may never be able to fully understand. It is the most mysterious of all aspects of our human identity. As advanced as our science is, we may only understand a miniscule fraction of the human brain's potential, its developmental needs or the assistance or harm we may be doing to it throughout our lives. Our new brain, the mind that is shaped by environmental forces such as television and other electronic media, may be operating within a set of circumstances of which we have no understanding and little concern for their potential impact on our species.

The focus on a rational, scientific, non-mythological paradigm has become the way of the modern world. This type of horizontal brain has become so prevalent that it dominates the western world—if not the entire globe. Take for example the political leaders who are confronted with a conflict between cultures they do not understand. President George W. Bush saw the Afghani and Iraqi cultures as a single entity, with oppositional qualities that did not partake in his religious belief system. He did not seek to learn their mythology. He made the decision to send troops and bombs to kill them, take over their countries and attempt to bring his accepted answer (democracy, Christianity) to their lands. I believe horizontal thinking dominated the plans for the second Gulf War and justified the rationalizations about weapons of mass destruction and other threats that reasoned it. Perhaps we were ready to accept such horizontal thoughts because of our predisposition to them.

In my opinion, the abandonment of mythological beliefs has strong implications for political, economic and social change everywhere. I learned how far-reaching America's electronic culture has become during my experience of traveling to the deepest depths of the Peruvian rainforest in the late 1990s. There I attended a local festival held by the indigenous population to celebrate the end of the rainy season. Strung over the mud streets of the main thoroughfare in the village was a sign, written in Spanish, announcing the festival:

WELCOME TO THE FESTIVAL OF JUAN DE BAPTISTA:
SPONSORED BY XEROX

Later during the trip, I went to the famed Inca ruins of Macchu Picchu. Here, two local beer companies had set up sponsorship and erected beer tents right on top of what had once likely been the spot of

Inca holy ceremonies. The horizontal mind has invaded the rainforest, the mountaintops, the first and third worlds and all of the lands in between.

The Symbol Language

The human brain has a miraculous ability to attach deep, resonating emotional connections to symbol language. I teach kids in high school about symbols in literature by asking them to look around the classroom and identify three symbols and their representative meaning. Often they will note the United States flag and its representation of democracy or freedom; they might even recall that the thirteen stripes represent the original colonies. Many identify the clock on the wall as a symbol of time, its most literal representation, and some even note its symbolic reference to life's passing and stages. Some astute students will even identify the computers in the room as symbols of progress or innovation. Most of the kids, and many of us adults, can understand these symbols.

But beyond literal symbolism lies the higher meaning of things in our world. The brain's miraculous ability is to take the abstract, attach deep, extensive and complex meaning to it and apply that meaning in many contexts on multiple levels simultaneously. This is how higher learning occurs: by taking the abstract and making it concrete, by taking the figurative and making the literal, not by identification but through interpretation and application of this transference. Programmed learning, which comes from memorization or learning that is dumped into the person from outside, is the weakest form of knowledge. Knowledge of symbols or, better said, the application of symbolic meaning, is one of the highest forms of knowledge.

William Carlos Williams said:

No ideas but in things!

Many of us have deep connections to political and religious symbols, such as the Berlin Wall, the Nazi Swastika, the cross, the Temple on the Mount and so on. Symbols and metaphors can have very meaningful connections if used in a measured process and if they are received by a brain that has developed the language structures to handle them. Poets know this process of applying emotional resonance to the concrete symbol very well. Writers like William Heyen take an abstract idea, such as extinction, which threatens many of the earth's species and quite literally means the end of all living things, and attach a deep and resonate level of meaning to it by using a small symbol, perhaps a bird, such as a passenger pigeon:

The Pigeons
By William Heyen
Audobon watched the flocks beat by for days
and tried, but could not count them:
their dung fell "like melting flakes of snow,"
the air buzzed until he lost his senses.

He heard, he said, their coo
and kee when they courted, and saw trees
of hundreds of nests, each cradling two
"broadly elliptical pure white eggs."

Over mast, they swept in "rich deep purple
circles," then roosted so thick that high limbs
cracked, and the pigeons avalanched
down the boughs, and had not room to fly,

and died by thousands. Kentucky farmers
fed their hogs on birds
knocked out of the air with poles. No net, stone,
arrow or bullet could miss one,

so horses drew wagons of them,
and schooners sailed cargoes of them,
and locomotives pulled freight cars of them
to the cities where they sold for one cent each.

When you touched one, its soft
feathers fell away as easily as a puff
of dandelion seeds, and its delicate breast-
bone seemed to return the pulse of your thumb.

Poems like this meld the worlds of science and art and move the brain to do what it can, if prodded enough and absent the preprogrammed repetition of horizontal learning: achieve higher meaning; meaning that matters, that resonates experientially and that coerces people to change and their brains to grow.

Heyen has written poems that both *do* this and *say* this at the same time in a near-perfect blend of the two minds:

On an Archaic torso of Apollo (after Rilke)

We cannot experience that storied head
in which Apollo's eyeballs ripened like apples. Yet
his torso glows, candelabra by
whose beams his gaze, though screwed back low,

still persists, still shines. Or else his breast's
curve would never blind you, nor his loins'
slight arc smile toward center-god, where
sperm seems candled from under.

Or else this stone would squat short, mute,
disfigured under the shoulders' translucent fall,
nor flimmer the black light of a beast's pelt, nor

break free of its own ideas
like a star. For here there is nothing nowhere
does not see you, charge you: You must change your life.

The important meaning of such poems is symbolic. Many have come out and said in public, "Extinction is wrong and must be stopped" or "Stop genocide; never let it happen again!" These things are said bluntly and loudly, over and over. But how much meaning is attached to them? We know that extinction and genocide are wrong, but they continue to happen in seemingly progressive ways all around us. We can say that this is evidence that the human brain has stopped evolving in symbolic directions and has turned outward, toward the literal, which does not resonate at the same levels and thus does not inspire us to change.

From an evolutionary perspective, we know that the brain's highest functions are challenged and come alive when a person is interpreting, analyzing and configuring the world around them through a combination of artistic and scientific thought processes—a function researchers call "blending." Poetry is one of the best examples of the brain's deep and focused concentration on the world around us. Walt Whitman composed a folio of poems about how keen observance of particular nature stimulates the learning process and development of the whole human on all levels:

I celebrate myself, and sing myself,
And what I assume you shall assume,
For every atom belonging to me as good belongs to you.

(From *Song of Myself*, 1855)

Whitman made an experiential oneness with the world's "original energy" by "observing a spear of summer grass." His observation of nature and humanity ushered in a new appreciation for close observation in American literature and the American mind. Much like a scientist placing small objects in front of his microscope lens, such poets saw power and spiritual glory in the details of nature. These were days of conflict and civil war, but they were also times dominated by an awareness of nature. The majority of Americans (although this was in the process of changing) were still working for, or in some sort of service to, agrarian ideals. Fathers still worked the plow with their sons; family life still centered on the home, in many cases the farm. People had time and reason to observe "a spear of summer grass." These were days when neural blooms were concentrated on vertical development instead of horizontal economics. It was a time when the blending phenomenon in the American brain was lopsided toward the aesthetic over the pragmatic.

The poet Albert Goldbarth once wrote,

> *Now when Moses went to the mountains to hear the Word, God needed to speak to him through a medium—the bush. And even from this, Moses needed to turn his face, or be blinded. The bush was a cover version of glory. There is a radiance so great, its being glimpsed will scorch our seeing forever. There is a pain so intense, direct contact will cripple, irremediably. There is a joy so numinous, to know it is to lose touch with this world. There is a thought so new, so strange, it will make of the mind another thing completely. For these the poem is a cover version. (Heyen, The Generation of 2000: Contemporary American Poets)*

Goldbarth makes clear that the vertical mindedness of the poem, the figurative quality over the literal, as intense and powerful as it may be, is but a cheap knockoff of the real thing—the transformational experience. Conversely, only if the brain is properly prepared with language nurtured during its childhood developmental phases can it accept and dwell within the poem, or within any artistic realm, or ever hope to receive the figurative transformations of the original "radiance" of the experience it represents. The brain can only accept transcendence, a transcendence which may, in fact, be evolutionary growth, if it is able to shed the diminishing effects of the brain's shutoff valve: electronic media. The trend toward the pragmatic mind that we have witnessed in the recent centuries is the valve turning the flow of development to the off position.

Henry David Thoreau made a lifestyle of these natural observations. And his fellow transcendentalists, and poets of all historic eras, spent their lives providing conditions in which the neocortex could strive for higher development. Thoreau said, "Shall I not have intelligence with the earth? Am I not partly leaves and vegetable mould myself?" He maintained an awareness that man is not separate from nature, but can only live successfully as part of it, both in a physical sense and in a psychic sense. He realized how important it is to create organic conditions in one's life that allow for upward psychic and brain development. The transcendentalist movement knew that true intelligence did not center in pragmatism alone, but in humans' relationship to the natural world.

The human brain developed in such a way as to achieve a natural oneness with nature, resulting in a sort of organic language processing system. But when the brain transfers these symbols to the neocortex, amazing things happen. All of the intuitive powers of the brain's system, along with the emotional powers that make human cognition so superior to all other forms of animal life, come into play, possess the symbols and join them with imagery. The brain's ability to process and create imagery is one of its strongest capabilities. More importantly, the brain uses metaphors, symbols and imagery to bring about states of being that differ from, or did not exist before, these cognitive processes. What poets, philosophers and theologians have called "higher meaning" are the brain's image mechanisms placing connotation to symbol.

Symbol language carries the ability to adjust for both bold and subtle states of awareness. Many people have deep levels of feelings about democracy and American values, for example. But rarely are these feelings so personified as when visitors walk across a symbolic setting such as the Pearl Harbor Memorial in Hawaii or stand before the eternal flame at the tomb of John F. Kennedy at Arlington National Cemetery. These symbols bring about far more than a pragmatic, horizontal understanding of democracy.

To assume that all symbols carry the same value in terms of the brain's capacity to link them with meaning is like assuming that a boy's slingshot and a nuclear missile are equally dangerous weapons. In the world of education, for example, we routinely diminish certain forms of symbols—poetry being a prevalent example—because the world sees few practical applications. But at the same time, educators are emphasizing symbol systems that are mathematically based and have few of the metaphorical empowerments of other language forms. Interpreting abstract symbols is one of the brain's highest functions. Mathematical applications, scientific formulas and computer codes are some of the most concrete symbols utilized in the educational marketplace, yet they are the most emphasized. Even in the English language classrooms where I have taught, the state's curriculum is profoundly based in business writing and other very pragmatic, practical applications. The New York State Regents Examination in English, for example, contains one full task dedicated to the interpretation of graphs, charts, tables and diagrams that explain a nonfiction topic. Fully one half of the examination is based on nonfiction, business-oriented communications. Past years' examinations have utilized data-based topics such as work related injuries, hurricane damage in Central America and adolescent sleep patterns. The symbol languages required for such tasks are hardly abstract, but in fact linear, practical, scientific—the essence of the horizontal mind.

Indigenous cultures have never had a problem with permanent adolescence, which may have something to do with their artistic interpretation of the world. Primal peoples view art far differently than modern westerners. To many primal cultures, there is no such thing as art and no word ot term for it in their original language. This is because the mystical perception of the world is the only perception of the world, and the realist view of Europeans does not exist. To many primal people, what we think of as art is a combination of factors that make up reality. If we were to pick this reality apart, we would probably call it part religion, part philosophy, part political. But to the Native American, for example, such divisions are meaningless. Art is simply the way things are.

A good example of this primal worldview is the depictions of animals displayed at many archeological sights. In these paintings the animals sometimes conform to the realistic image of the mammal, but often such realities are not adhered to. The artists seemed only concerned with showing what art historian Herbert Read called, "the essence of the animal." Some were drawn as part human, with two human legs and a human chest but with a deer head and antlers. Others were grossly disproportioned, discolored or otherwise ornate. The primal artists took their experiences with nature, a reality in which they were already personally and culturally entwined, and depicted them as such with no separation. Like the hunt itself, there were some days when the game was evasive, others when it was plentiful. The animals had their own mythological traits, such as aggressiveness, cunningness or benevolence, and these were represented in the images as well. Much of the art created during the later Paleolithic was reserved for the very back recesses of the caves and caverns. Some of it could only be reached by crawling on hands and knees down an intricate path. This tells us that the primal artists used their creations for sacred purposes and divine communication, not for entertainment. Apparently, the people of the Paleolithic saw little distinction between the animal and its artistic representation. Paintings on the cave wall were sacred, as was the animal itself.

We can say that in the perception of art, there are really two minds, much like we have proposed in the biological makeup of the brain or in the philosophical protocol of our reality. One of which are those whose consciousness allows for primal, mythological, organic aesthetics and the other are those who do not. The Western sensibility drifted toward realism quite early on and has stayed that way except for a few forays into the abstract. This new pragmatic reality has firmly planted itself in the Western mind and, like a crop of weeds, has grown to take over the entire field. Modern art is an extension of this, with its noticeable lack of sacredness. In America's art schools, the pragmatic mind drives students to pursue careers in web design, become business managers at museums or help advertise products in mass media. In the Western world, art and commerce have become one, and art has lost its purpose.

Mark Turner, a highly distinguished professor of linguistics and mathematics, has dutifully researched the mental spaces that combine scientific and artistic thought—a phenomenon that he calls "conceptual blending" or "cognitive blending." Blending, says Turner, is a higher order of cognitive operation that developed during the evolutionary window during the Upper Paleolithic, sometime between 40,000 and 17,000 B.C. Developing the conceptual blending trait may have been the one cognitive evolutionary process, more important than language development, more important than emotion, that allowed for the greatest leap in human innovation. The ability to blend the scientific and the artistic, the aesthetic with the practical, in a unified dimension allowed human beings to pursue art, science, religion, culture, tools and most of the institutions we think of today as defining human civilization. Blending may also be notable because it provides a workspace in the brain for symbolic language, including the invention of mythology and artistic symbols, as well as scientific achievement. In other words, blending acts with a synergistic effect, propelling both regions of cognition to new heights that neither can achieve autonomously.

Turner says that blending takes place in the background and is thus invisible to the consciousness. Its mission and process is to take complex, abstract ideas—often those that diverge—and make unified sense of them, finally yielding a cognitive product. Without the ability to blend, the human brain could reason, but would have no emotional attachment; we could reproduce, but never bind together in love. The blending characteristic allows for virtually all of what is now thought of as the great human achievements: family, creativity, invention, literature, judgment, reasoning and language, to name but a few.

Blending

We have discussed the two minds: the horizontal and the vertical. Language scholars are now studying this division as well, and many theories have come forth in recent years to explain the division, sort out the parts of the brain that may be linked to the two minds, and determine the best ways to stimulate growth in these areas. Most everyone seems to agree that blending the scientific and artistic is mandatory for advanced thought and that one galaxy of the brain cannot progress without consideration from the other. Blending, they say, is the trait that allows the human species to think on a literal and figurative level simultaneously; it is the one trait that allowed us to take a giant leap forward in evolution—and restoring the right blend may be the only way to make further evolutionary progress.

Our premise is that the human mind thinks in stories. To sort out any problem, large or small, we tend to think in applications and theoretical examples. Take the case of the Chinese engineers who recently built the massive Three Gorges Dam on the Yangzi River in China. They could not go out and build such a dam without first contemplating the water needs of the region, the energy supply needs of the nation, the cost, the impact on people in the region, the rice farmer whose land will be flooded and so on. Addressing complex problems takes a blend of artistry and emotion as well as science and math. Our weekly trip to the grocery store is another example of blending at work. We don't go to the store and buy food without first envisioning its taste, its smell, the price or what dish we might later use it in; we consider whether or not we already have the ingredient at home, and we may even think of the person or company that produced the food product and evaluate their reputation as well. So, too, the human mind gravitates toward such application stories in its natural, or organic, course of thinking. Psychologists sometimes call this phenomenon "projection;" they say one of its functions is to help us visualize the impact of our theoretical actions before they are actually implemented. The brain's ability to blend story and the abstract with the practical, concrete application is the sincere genius of the human species and the thing that separates us from every other life form on earth. Many of the problems humans face today may be a factor of our brains' growing inability to blend the figurative with the practical before we make decisions. Many rice farmers' lands have been flooded in recent years by dam projects; many bombs have been dropped on innocent families; many people, animals and things destroyed, possibly because we have not been able to think in the metaphorical way that would have allowed us to foresee the consequences of our decisions, or at least empathize with the victims.

When we speak of the vertical and horizontal minds and the blending phenomenon, we should look at them as two cultures that are distinct yet interdependent. Like human cultures, the story side of the brain contains more than one cognitive ethnicity; it includes analogy, metaphor, symbol, mythology, metonymy, emotion and many other forms of abstract and metaphysical dialogues that resist encapsulation. This group forms the vertical mind. The other equator of the mind, the horizontal or concrete side, is made up of distinctly opposite processes. It is stoic, linear, unemotional, application-oriented and rooted in conservative work—work that believes that whatever concept is currently on the table will have a definitive, finite resolution as well as a practical application. When the horizontal mind thinks of building a dam, it thinks in pounds of concrete, truckloads of rebar, cost of labor and so forth. The two cultures are not political opponents, however, like the Republican and Democratic parties in the United States, but are more like two separate tribes whose cultural borders share some common hunting ground.

Recent research on the human brain is beginning to tell us two very important things in terms of cognitive blending at this time and place in human history. First, we understand that the process of blending is always a joint operation. That is, the brain cannot first contemplate the figurative and then go back and consider the practical. The two happen at once, although to different degrees. One cannot say to one's self on any particular day, "Oh, it's Tuesday. Today I am going to think vertically and just use my artistic mind." We are incapable of such choice, mainly because our brain structures have developed to operate in two modes simultaneously and without competition. Second, to develop one of the two cognitive cultures so that it completely dominates the other may be the most detrimental thing possible in terms of human development. Such changes are, unfortunately, occurring right now, on both a developmental scale—over the course of each person's lifetime—and on an evolutionary scale—over the course of many generations.

Although blending was present, the aesthetic culture of the vertical mind was the dominant cognitive trait for almost all human history. We can trace the use of mythology, art and story back to the earliest human tribes, and archeologists have proven that artistic creation and mythology played a central role in even the earliest documented cultures. Many scholars have written about the role of art in humanity, and most seem to agree that its role was dominant throughout the evolutionary history of our people, at least in terms of its cultural impact, until very recent times. But today, in just a millisecond of evolutionary time, the dominance of the vertical mind has subsided, and the blend has become so imbalanced in favor of the horizontal mind that our entire evolutionary scope has changed. There was a confluence of events at about the time of the Industrial Revolution when John Dewey and his colleagues ushered in the era of pragmatism, and the balance shifted dramatically. We might say that the human way of thinking and reasoning is a martini that was once four parts vertical gin. But recently the recipe has changed; horizontal vermouth became the dominant ingredient, and the bite of the gin has given way to a sweeter tasting but ultimately more destructive cocktail.

If, as the Paleolithic dawned the blending trait appeared in the human brain, what is the status of brain evolution during our present era, the Holocene? Where is the human brain headed? This, of course, is the ultimate question. What cognitive traits will arise tomorrow, and which will subside and become useless in the new millennium? Because our cognitive evolution no longer takes place in an organic environment, we can assume that the non-organic factors that dominate our lives are steering evolutionary brain development in their direction. We continue to adapt, as evolution intends, but we are adapting to a new world, a world dominated by a branch of human evolution gone badly astray.

Part ②

Fathers and Sons

⑥

A Child's Story

Charles Dickens paid special attention to the place of children in the world. He knew firsthand the struggles of young men in the emerging industrial society of Europe in the 1800s. His treatment of boys in his writing often takes on a pitying dimension, such as the Tiny Tim character in *A Christmas Carol*. However, his short stories can also help us understand the initiation rituals and, particularly, symbols that afterward were missing from the coming-of-age experience during the industrial revolution in Europe and America.

One widely published version of Dickens' *The Child's Story* illustrates this point.

> *Once upon a time, a good many years ago, there was a traveller, and he set out upon a journey. It was a magic journey, and was to seem very long when he began it, and very short when he got half way through.*

The title and introduction indicate that the story is about childhood and adolescent development. On reading, we find the traveler in the tale seems to be fully grown, but he is adventuresome like a child. We know this because the journey is called a "magic journey." All of us, men and women, no matter how horrible the period of time, remember our adolescent moments as being at least on some level "magical." What other word perfectly describes the first discovery of sexuality, of intense emotions such as compassion and fear? Often, children think to themselves at the onset of adolescence, "Have I gone mad?" They might fall in love with their math teacher or, looking in the mirror one morning, find a blemish on their cheek that moves them to tears. The "magic" of adolescence is not the physical change, but the emotional reaction that ebbs and flows like the strongest tide.

Dickens also describes the boy as being on a journey that is both very long and very short. Many men among us remember their adolescence as both of those things. Most importantly, we know that the boy is on a journey, a real journey of importance, a literal journey and a figurative journey. What better metaphor could there be for the experience? We have talked about some of the physical and symbolic journeys adolescents feel they need to endure in order to make their way through the experience. In some cultures, even today, like boys who journey unprotected into the forest for several days, and children throughout America who embark on journeys with the U.S. military when they are still in adolescence, engage in a physical journey as a rite of passage. The American Amish culture has the ritual of Rumskalla, when teenagers are sent out to experience the world and, hopefully, return to the church for the same purpose. It is a way to purposefully identify their independence from the family and recognize their own life skills, which they have been working on for some time. Dickens' story continues:

> He travelled along a rather dark path for some little time, without meeting anything, until at last he came to a beautiful child. So he said to the child, "What do you do here?" And the child said, "I am always at play. Come and play with me!"

Children learn, develop and express themselves through play. It is their main method of communication. Adults, however, must forsake playfulness, bite into the apple of seriousness and duty, go to college, get a job and assume responsibility, so their play mechanism is shut off quite early. Dickens seems interested in this idea because he begins the next part of the story by saying:

> *So he played with that child, the whole day long, and they were very merry. The sky was so blue, the sun was so bright, the water was so sparkling, the leaves were so green, the flowers were so lovely, and they heard such singing birds and saw so many butterflies, that everything was beautiful. This was in fine weather. When it rained, they loved to watch the falling drops, and to smell the fresh scents. When it blew, it was delightful to listen to the wind…*

We see here that the older man, the traveler, has regained an original relationship with nature. Like the indigenous cultures around the world that have this mythological relationship with their environment, the traveler has regained this experience through the child, who has yet to lose it. All mythology originates in explanations and relationships with nature, so it is no surprise that the very first revelation in the story is that of the man finding the wholeness of the sparkling water, the lovely flowers and the joyfulness of the whipping wind so fulfilling. The traveler and the child even find ecstasy in a blizzard when they notice, "white flakes falling fast and thick, like down from the breasts of millions of white birds."

This original experience of the world that the child in the story has and shares with the older man is one that can be described as psychic awareness or organic wholeness. It is a state of being that babies are born with, prior to the time when their minds become clouded with what poet Allen Ginsberg once called, "the dirty dishwater of other people's thinking." It is the mind that Zen meditation strives to reach, the poet's mind. Buddhists call this place *nirvana*; all religions know of it. Mountaineers sometimes speak of this state when they are high on a ridge with nothing but the hum of wilderness all around. For modern adults, if we work hard enough, on the meditation pillow or climbing up the mountain, we may be lucky enough to have a glance of this original mind for an instant. But the traveler in the story has regained the original mind by proximity. We get the feeling that he has struggled for some time in a busy life, perhaps in an office cubicle or at an engineer's computer monitor, and has had a tremendous weight removed through his experience with nature at the hands of the child. There's something ecstatic here and a definite sense of relief.

Dickens seems to recognize a complex evolutionary contradiction. It is really a battle between the forces of instinct—what we have previously called the original mind/organic wholeness—and the horizontal thinking that the digital world is so predicated on. Instinctual forces deal in the realm of nature, the world the boy and his companion find so meaningful and rewarding. The horizontal world, the one where so many of us reside today, is the world of television and cellular telephones. It is a place that is becoming less and less reliant on instinct and more and more dependent on analysis, practicality, engineering and systems invented by mankind to make nature less relevant…systems such as highways, televisions, school districts, factories and other consumer enterprises.

We know that the original mind relies upon nature to interpret its world. Ancient cave paintings, Greek temples and Egyptian tombs all display a willful reverence of nature. But in the digital world, the world of evangelism and capitalist economics, nature is our enemy. Forests are barriers to the new subdivision; the national park is preventing a new copper mine; the coasts of Alaska must be invaded and drilled so that we can add fuel to the supply system and drop gasoline prices to stay economically competitive with China. And so on.

The brain that has become reliant on the digital world is no longer comfortable in nature. We have chosen to place the once wild animals in zoos, on calendars or on television specials so that we can see them from a safe distance. In one generation, we stamp out all of the predators from places like Yellowstone Park and the Adirondack Mountains; the next generation tries to replant a few wolves in the Yellowstone caldera or a few Condors in the Grand Canyon so that we can ensure our control of nature is complete. We can destroy it, then bring it back if we so choose, but in limited quantities and in places of our choosing. It is an attitude well-parodied in Michael Crichton's novel *Jurassic Park,* where scientists re-create an extinct race of dinosaurs *because they can.* Alston Chase wrote about the very real control of nature in his book, *Playing God in Yellowstone,* and Bill McKibben took a sobering look at the next step in *The End of Nature.* Quite a few people are currently working in cloning laboratories to genetically replicate everything from one-celled organisms to human beings so that we can manage the traits of future generations. The horizontal culture seems to very deeply enjoy its domination of the natural world.

It is interesting to note that the older man in Dickens' story is apt to not only accept, but also revel in the child's fascination with nature and determination at play. Most parents recognize the joy in playing with their toddler. However, rarely can a parent take hour upon hour or day upon day of nonstop play with the same tolerance. On the other hand, among the birds, bears and wolverines of the wilderness, adults seem to resolutely accept their roles in the lives of their children without frustration. In this way we can almost call the older man in Dickens' story *animal-like.*

But, one day, of a sudden, the traveller lost the child. He called to him over and over again, but got no answer. So, he went upon his road, and went on for a little while without meeting anything, until at last he came to a handsome boy. So, he said to the boy, "What do you do here?" And the boy said, "I am always learning. Come and learn with me."

The adult in the story has experienced the end of the first stage of development in the child. It is the death of the child's original mind. No longer experiencing the world as miraculous rain, wind and nature, he is now able to learn and evaluate his surroundings. He is excited by this change. We can hear the eagerness in his voice when he invites the man to "Come and *learn* with me."

Children are thrilled when they realize that they are able to learn new things. Tying shoes, saying new words, building towers with blocks are all milestones recognized by the child as well as the parent. But the child, unlike the parent, somewhere in the back of his mind, also has a realization that aside from something new that is now growing in him, something else has died. The death of the original mind is perhaps the most important aspect of this stage of life, for the memory of it lingers for a long time, well into adulthood. Many of us spend the rest of our lives trying to recapture it.

Psychoanalyst Sigmund Freud said that the death of the original mind occurs at birth. He felt that the child's transportation down the birth canal and into the state of breathing without an umbilical chord is the death of the original mind and a shattering experience that leaves trauma in its wake. But the baby, perhaps until about fifteen months or so, before language and motor skills and cerebral cortex development really take hold, is still enjoying the freedom that Dickens wrote about in the first part of the story. The adults care for the baby. His food is delivered, his temperature kept comfortable with blankets and furnace; he is doted over. The problem really comes when his mind is able to evaluate his surroundings and he has to decide, "Do I want spinach today? No, I don't!" These decisions and the learning that they entail are the first conflicts in the child's life. The ability to learn and evaluate decisions independently provides an opportunity for the death of the original mind in the learning stage.

So he learned with that boy about Jupiter and Juno, and the Greeks and the Romans, and I don't know what, and learned more than I could tell—or he either,

for he soon forgot a great deal of it. But, they were not always learning; they had
the merriest games that ever were played. They rowed upon the river in summer,
and skated on the ice in winter; they were active afoot, and active on horseback;
at cricket, and all games at ball; at prisoner's base, hare and hounds, follow my
leader, and more sports than I can think of; nobody could beat them. They had
holidays too, and Twelfth cakes, and parties where they danced till midnight, and
real Theatres where they saw palaces of real gold and silver rise out of the real
earth, and saw all the wonders of the world at once. As to friends, they had such
dear friends and so many of them, that I want the time to reckon them up. They
were all young, like the handsome boy, and were never to be strange to one another
all their lives through.

Dickens, who knew full well the tribulations of childhood from firsthand experience, focuses this section of the story on the joyful awakening of the learning stage. The ecstatic joyfulness of it comes from the fact that not only are the pedagogical steps original, but also the content of the learning is new. Remember, if you can, the first time you played ball, the first time you played follow-the-leader, your first holiday. These experiences resonate particularly because the original mind, even if it has been killed off or injured, is still recent enough to provide a context. By the time the boy is thirty, he still remembers his first holiday, but the original mind is so far gone that it has little impact relative to the four-year-old.

It is also interesting to notice that in this stage of maturation, the man and the boy begin to see gold and silver. Dickens takes pains to say, "they saw places of real gold and silver rise out of the earth." He places the word *real* in the sentence very carefully, very particularly. He wants the reader to see that the shining brightness of the experience is like the glimmer of *real* gold and *real* silver, not something cheap and mass-produced, but something genuine. It is worth noting as well that at the time of this writing, Europe was being overtaken by the Industrial Revolution. Belching factories and smokestacks were devouring London, and the connection to the *real earth*, as Dickens puts it, was in the process of being destroyed by the gears of mechanization. He seems to be saying in this part of the story that this stage of development in the boy is a stage where he should be learning about nature, perhaps coupling it with the knowledge of nature planted in the original mind.

The man and the boy have now become somewhat synonymous, even though their relationship has only spanned a paragraph or so. They are discussed as a unit. This can only be seen as a definition of the mentor-student relationship that was once so important to young men. Moreover, Dickens says their social circle is filling up, that they have "such dear friends and so many of them." Ages three through five is when children begin to understand socialization, social rank and meaningful friendship. Dickens puts great emphasis on the friends made at this age. He says they will remain friends their whole lives through because of the beauty of their shared experience.

The story goes on like a roller coaster, much like life. The boy and the man are happy. They have reached maturational stages that are filled with beauty and knowledge, but they are not to last.

> Still, one day, in the midst of all these pleasures, the traveller lost the boy as he had lost the child, and, after calling to him in vain, went on upon his journey. So he went on for a little while without seeing anything, until at last he came to a young man. So, he said to the young man, "What do you do here?" And the young man said, "I am always in love. Come and love with me."

> So, he went away with that young man, and presently they came to one of the prettiest girls that ever was seen… So, the young man fell in love directly…and [they] were engaged at Christmas-time, and sat close to one another by the fire, and were going to be married very soon…

It is important to ask some questions at this point in the story. Who is this boy and who is this man? We can assume that the many boys in the story are really the same boy at different stages. Clearly the boy is alone; we can assume he is an orphan. Like so many modern, industrialized children, his father has gone off to another place—the factory, drugs, women, early death, whatnot. The boy has been left to fend for himself in the world. Yet there's a modicum of celebration going on in the boy. Why?

Many of us who have lost our fathers to the forces of the industrial society rejoice to an extent because we blame our fathers for not being there for us. This hidden (and sometimes not so hidden) animosity is well justified in a child who knows nothing but a sense of abandonment. Culturally, as well, there was a sense of piousness when the patriarchy began to fall apart. But we are now realizing that the problem is much broader than we first gathered. We are beginning to understand that the father did not destroy himself, but was killed by destructive forces far larger than even he could understand. Like a small stick caught up in the swirling winds of a hurricane, the patriarchy was carried off and disappeared. Worse still, the forces that destroyed him have also turned their sights on the mother.

Mythologically (not to mention practically), the mother is the planet on which we live. Is it not a resolute understanding by now that with all we know about climate change, wilderness destruction and the impact of toxic chemicals and fossil fuels on the air, sea and land, she is in fact dying, if not dead to us already? If the patriarch died with the industrial revolution and the matriarch is on her deathbed now, what can we call the child who is left? We must call him—us—"orphan" like the boy in our story.

Now we come to the point in the maturational journey when the boy is first referred to as a young man. His attention has turned from matters of play to matters of love and lust. But remember, the boy in the story is an orphan; he has no one to teach him about women and relationships. His emotions run high, but he has no understanding of how to deal with them. He is like the high school boy who gets in trouble at school for wearing his hat when he's not supposed to. When he's called down to the principal's office, instead of apologizing and moving on, he becomes furious and punches the principal in the face and is hauled off to jail. I see it time and time again in the schools. Some young men are furious or falling apart emotionally because of relationships with young women that didn't go well. But unlike in the past when they would take their feelings home and discuss them with their fathers, mothers or maybe older brothers, today they punch their hand through windows, steal cars and drive the vehicles drunk into a row of trees, find guns and do something terrible with them or sock the principal. More and more are committing suicide or attempting it. Like the boy obsessed with the girl in the story, our male teens today do not have a support structure to help them understand their emotions and make reasonable decisions. We can sense something disastrous about to happen to Dickens' boy in his haste to get engaged.

> But, the traveller lost them one day, as he had lost the rest of his friends, and, after calling to them to come back, which they never did, went on upon his journey. So, he went on for a little while without seeing anything, until at last he came to a middle-aged gentleman. So, he said to the gentleman, "What are you doing here?" And his answer was, "I am always busy. Come and be busy with me!"

> So, he began to be very busy with that gentleman, and they went on through the wood together. The whole journey was through a wood, only it had been open and green at first, like a wood in spring; and now began to be thick and dark, like a wood in summer; some of the little trees that had come out earliest, were even turning brown. The gentleman was not alone, but had a lady of about the same age with him, who was

his Wife; and they had children, who were with them too. So,
they all went on together through the wood, cutting down the
trees, and making a path through the branches and the fallen
leaves, and carrying burdens, and working hard.

A funny thing has happened here and it has to do, I think, with tone. There is usually an ecstatic tone surrounding children. We love them, even when they are sometimes difficult and misbehave, even if they are not ours by birth. We value children because there is something holy and original in them—they are genuine humans without the pretense of adults, without the "dirty dishwater of other people's thinking." We sense here in the story that there has been a shift. We sensed it was coming when we heard about the boy's affair and engagement. That's when parents feel it as well. Anyone who has a son or daughter who has gone on a first date can attest to that. But at this point in the life of a child, there's a mythological experience as well, one that goes back to the earliest beliefs—in life and death. Here we have experienced the death of the boy's childhood and the birth of his adulthood. He must go out into the world and make his living, experience independence, provide for a wife and children. This is hard work indeed, both psychically and physically. It is a turning point that in tribal societies would have necessitated a ceremony of some type.

I think Dickens was especially sensitive to this part of life because of his own difficult childhood. His father was a businessman, somewhat prosperous, who aspired to be more than what he was capable of. He mismanaged the family's funds and, in a collapse when Dickens was a young man, was thrown into the poorhouse, along with his suffering wife and his son. Young Dickens was forced to work countless hours in the sprouting London factories under the supervision of heartless bosses in order to help pay off the family's debt. It was an experience that in effect ended his childhood and thrust him into the world of working men and women. Both *Oliver Twist* and *A Christmas Carol* owe to the burden of this part of Europe's history. The villain Fagin in *Oliver Twist*, for example, is said to have been modeled after one of the cruel, older boys who worked over Dickens in a shoe polish factory.

In many original cultures and throughout mythology, the passing of childhood is marked like a death, with mourning and ceremony, but also with a sense of celebration. In the Christian literature, there is the marking of Jesus' final day on earth before he is to go to his duty at the hands of the Romans. At the last supper, Mathew, Mark, John, Paul and the men of the circle walk out into the garden. But instead of somber prayer, Jesus takes their hands in a circle and sings, "Glory be to Thee, Father!" It is a joyful moment, just before Jesus goes to his death.

The Egyptians, as is well documented, worshiped Osiris, who was both the lord of the dead and the lord of the regeneration of life. Thus there is continuity between the loss of life, the loss of one part of a boy's life and the birth of another. The occasion is seen throughout history as a transcendent experience; a difficult, but joyous experience, for birth is always joyous, even under the most difficult of circumstances.

I once visited my sister in South America while she was working as a medical missionary. We took a small boat down the Amazon River from the Peruvian frontier town of Iquitos to a small jungle village on the banks of the Amazon called Gaillito. Once there, the village elder came to meet us; he promptly informed us that there was no time for greeting—a village woman was about to deliver a baby, it was getting dark and what were we waiting for? My sister rolled up her sleeves and went to work with the woman in the small medical hut on the riverbank. The sun went down quickly, as it does near the equator, and it grew pitch dark; flashlights were collected and brought to the hut, which had no electricity. I stayed outside, but went to see what was happening several times as the hours passed by. It was clearly a difficult delivery. I heard the woman scream over and over again as her contractions ebbed and flowed, and I wondered if she or the baby would die in childbirth because of a lack of equipment or medicine. After many hours of this, my sister emerged, cleaned herself up and announced that they had delivered a healthy baby girl.

"Is the mother alright?" I asked, noting the length of time that had passed and the horrible screaming that had been coming from the medical hut most of the night. Just as I asked, the mother and newborn emerged from the doorway. She was smiling as broadly as anyone possibly could have, heedless of the blood running down her legs and the torn sheet she was wearing. It was clearly an experience of pure ecstasy for her. I went to congratulate her the next day and, in my broken Spanish, asked if she was all right. I told her she sounded as though things had been quite difficult for her the night before.

"No. No," she responded. "The birth was beautiful."

This story illustrates how many cultures around the world believe that not just the baby, but the birth experience itself is a sacred thing. Pearce writes that in modern America we have taken a very wrong turn by opting to deliver babies in conditions that set the baby and mother at odds from the very beginning of their postpartum relationship. By delivering in barren, sterile, hospital rooms and by taking the baby away from the mother almost immediately after birth, he says, we may be doing far more psychological damage to the newborn than we realize.

We'll continue with Dickens' story a bit further:

Sometimes, they came to a long green avenue that opened into deeper woods. Then they would hear a very little, distant voice crying, "Father, father, I am another child! Stop for me!" And presently they would see a very little figure, growing larger as it came along, running to join them. When it came up, they all crowded round it, and kissed and welcomed it; and then they all went on together.

Sometimes, they came to several avenues at once, and then they all stood still, and one of the children said, "Father, I am going to sea," and another said, "Father, I am going to India," and another, "Father, I am going to seek my fortune where I can," and another, "Father, I am going to Heaven!" So, with many tears at parting, they went, solitary, down those avenues, each child upon its way; and the child who went to Heaven, rose into the golden air and vanished.

The traveler watches the gentleman at these partings, noticing his grey hair and the wood turning brown. Eventually, all the children depart, leaving the traveler and the gentleman and his wife to continue on their journey of being always busy.

At last the woman hears a voice calling her:

It was the voice of the first child who had said, "I am going to Heaven!" and the father said, "I pray not yet. The sunset is very near. I pray not yet!"

But, the voice cried, "Mother, mother!" without minding him, though his hair was now quite white, and tears were on his face.

Then, the mother, who was already drawn into the shade of the dark avenue and moving away with her arms still round his neck, kissed him, and said, "My dearest, I am summoned, and I go!" And she was gone. And the traveller and he were left alone together.

Journeying to the end of the wood, the traveler once again finds himself alone:

> *Yet, once more, while he broke his way among the branches, the traveller lost his friend. He called and called, but there was no reply, and when he passed out of the wood, and saw the peaceful sun going down upon a wide purple prospect, he came to an old man sitting on a fallen tree. So, he said to the old man, "What do you do here?" And the old man said with a calm smile, "I am always remembering. Come and remember with me!"*

So the traveller sat down by the side of that old man, face to face with the serene sunset; and all his friends came softly back and stood around him. The beautiful child, the handsome boy, the young man in love, the father, mother and children: every one of them was there, and he had lost nothing. So, he loved them

all, and was kind and forbearing with them all, and was always pleased to watch
them all, and they all honoured and loved him. And I think the traveller must be
yourself, dear Grandfather, because this what you do to us, and what we do to you.

It would be an oversimplification to say that the traveler in the story
is man and his companion is his inner child. But we wouldn't be exactly
wrong in this assessment either. We know that the field of psychology has
made marvelous advances in the past hundred years or so. The
understanding that one's childhood never fully leaves the psyche is one
of these great understandings. We all have an emotional connection to
our childhood, beyond just the memories represented by it.

Jungian Perspectives

Psychologist and psychiatrist Carl Jung made a pertinent observation
about the world of childhood and adults:

Under the influence of scientific materialism, everything that could not be seen
with the eyes or touched with the hands was held in doubt; such things were even
laughed at because of their supposed affinity with metaphysics. Nothing was
considered "scientific" or admitted to be true unless it could be perceived by the
senses or traced back to physical causes. This radical change of view did not begin
with philosophical materialism, for the way was being prepared long before. When
the spiritual catastrophe of the Reformation put an end to the Gothic Age with
its impetuous yearning for the heights, its geographical confinement and its
restricted view of the world, the vertical outlook of the European mind was
forthwith intersected by the horizontal outlook of modern times. Consciousness
ceased to grow upward, and grew instead in breadth of view, as well as in
knowledge of the terrestrial globe.

Jung understood the culture's developing reliance on the physical
senses in the industrial era. He also comments on the "scientific
materialism" that dominated during his time and remains dominate in

our own. Had he lived long enough, Jung would have not been surprised at the turn European and American culture has taken since the 1930s. Jung's postulates and condemnation of scientific thought was appropriate for his era, especially given the movement of the pragmatists at the time, namely William James and John Dewey and their followers. Jung saw his contemporaries in philosophy and in the culture at large as having begun a love affair with "other worldliness converted to matter-of-factness; empirical boundaries set to man's discussion of every problem," to a world where "no value exists if it is not founded on a so-called fact."

Jung's remorse was founded in his observation that "Today the psyche does not build itself a body, but on the contrary, matter, by chemical action, produces the psyche." We know that both physically and psychologically, things build upon things and structures build upon structures. It seems as though in Dickens' stories, the boy is out in the woods or traveling along the road trying to nurture his psyche. Psychic work is hard work, hard inner work. It involves confronting some very hard facts about the self, the identity and the world. To take a close look at one's self and one's ability, or lack thereof, even to look mortality in the eye, takes wild energy and deep bravery. "Building a psyche" from simple chemical action, from the random strokes of matter, requires much less work, much less determination and little bravery. Perhaps industrial society in Jung's time and, in our own, found a way to both increase economic prosperity and decrease the amount of exhausting inner work the psyche needs at the same time.

One of Jung's foundational beliefs dealt with the relationship between the conscious and unconscious minds, or what he termed the "dialogue between the ego and the self." He called this process "individualization" and thought it to be the single most important aspect of developing healthy individuals and avoiding psychological conflict and disorder. The Jungian "self" is the total person, including the conscious and the unconscious, the scientific and aesthetic, the physical and the emotional, the remnants of the original mind and the development of the new brain and its complex and developing connections. Jung found it troubling in his day that people were not much interested in doing inner work on their psyches and, moreover, that psychology at the time was growing increasingly focused on a "psychology without the psyche" that treated all thought as a biochemical process. An estimated 20 million Americans have at one time or another taken antidepressants, and that figure includes 1.7 million children who are currently on such medications. If he were alive today, Jung wouldn't be surprised at the frequency at which we prescribe antidepressants and other psychotropic drugs. We have, as he long ago predicted, given up on the inner self and pursued scientific alternatives to treat our inner disorders. Dickens reminds us that children still need to go about the wooded trails, and adults still need to go with them, if only to convince themselves that their psyches are still intact and dynamically woven into their lives.

Jung called out in his day for a field of psychological study that considered the psyche as its own divine entity, but that would have required science to admit to a phenomenon that is not quantifiable and whose physical attributes are nonexistent. His pragmatic contemporaries were aghast at such a proposition, but in children we can see the winged spirit of the psyche at work before the ego self has developed and begun to slather it with coverings. In children we can easily recognize the raw excitement and exuberance when they observe small things in nature— a bird, a leaf, a caterpillar. And as adults we have a psychic connection to the days of psychic energy whenever we see children with their original minds and original energies at work, their eyes wide at the sight of some new creature.

Entering the
Forbidden Room

Many modern psychological theories relate most everything to the mother's influence. Perhaps this is because both Freud and Jung were so maternally focused. Fathers, at least in the traditional view, have been away taking care of business while a female, the mother, provides child care. This view began to change during the feminist movement of the 1960s and 1970s, but it is still a deeply engrained idea. Perhaps we should take a moment to re-examine the patriarch's house and see what happens when the son's yearning for a father image is replaced by empty rooms that the male child often fills with media images, mythological creations and visions of his father's imagined life.

I first took a hard look at this when my father died at age eighty-seven. Three days after his death, my three sisters and I gathered for a service at the funeral home, and then took his ashes away in two containers. We drove to the shore of Lake Ontario, where we cast off the majority of the remains in a biodegradable disk, a contraption that looks to be made from two paper plates glued together with his ashes inside. It careened a little way offshore, filled with water on that cold and windy October day and sank to the bottom. My sisters didn't want to let the disc go. They were troubled by how close to shore it still was, that the ashes were not dissolving and floating away, that the container was not degrading quickly enough. They wanted to search for a stick or wade out into the surf to push the remains out farther in the tide. Finally, convinced that there was nothing more to be done, they relented.

We went to our next stop with a smaller pewter jar that contained the last, small physical remnant of our father. We drove to the cemetery where our mother is buried. She had died twenty-one years earlier, a cancer victim. She had been eighteen when she married my father. It was World War II; he was a pilot waiting to ship out to the war in the Pacific. As the story goes, they knew each other for only two weeks before they married. Times were different then. He abused her for much of their marriage. It was a long and complicated life together that encompassed five children, two separations, a divorce and reconciliation, a nine-year battle with cancer, the burial of their first-born son after a horrendous late-night car crash and a host of other joys and tragedies. Every family has a story to tell. In the end, they were together again and, as my father had wished, we sprinkled a bit of his ashes over her grave, laid down some flowers and returned to our lives.

My father was unique and different, but like many men of his generation and the present one, he lived in a dwelling that was as mysterious and empty as it was known and familiar. Most American fathers, as did mine, think that their life is different than that of their children. They assume that they have come from some far different place—perhaps it is even physically different, say, they are immigrants or grew up during the Great Depression, as my father did. "They just don't understand what it was like," they say to themselves and perhaps out loud once in a while. The son then grows up with a vacancy sign hung over the father's room, because they know their father believes his experience will never be understood. The father sees his son as ignorant, spoiled and unappreciative of his sacrifice, whatever it may be. This is a characteristic of my father's generation, but also of the present one and the ones that came before.

The son wakes up each morning as his father is leaving for work in the office or factory. When the father leaves the house, he hangs the vacancy sign up on his door and shuts his room up tight. The mother sends the son a troubled glance as the father leaves and the son is left wondering what it is about the father that cannot be explained. *What is the mystery?* becomes the undying question of the boy's youth.

When the father returns home at the end of the day, he is tired from work and from not being treated with the respect he feels he deserves. He has been grinding gears on a lathe, adding rows of figures or, like Charlie Bucket's father in Roald Dahl's *Charlie and the Chocolate Factory*, screwing tops onto toothpaste tubes all day. Maybe he is even doing a task that is more white-collar, like legal work or dentistry. Still, he becomes bitter, because he is working for a paycheck, trying to earn a living to care for his family, yet the place where he spends his energy is an office, an assembly line, a fire station or the operator's compartment of a backhoe. He leaves his commitment there and can bring little home except disappointment. His work is an abstraction to his son, unlike the agrarian world of the farmers of long ago. Meanwhile, the son is left to fill his father's room with mythology, imagined kings and the pieces of the propaganda puzzle his father has left on the floor. The son cannot simply step off the back porch and watch his father do his work. He must imagine the life his father leads and spends the majority of his energy on.

The Propaganda Shop

Sometimes, in place of the vacancy sign the father hangs on his door as he leaves the house, he may leave a sign that means: Propaganda Shop: Come In! The son has pieces of a puzzle to work with. The father tells the son things about his work life. Usually they are exaggerations meant to show the son that he is a hero—the type of hero definition the son has learned from television, children's stories and video games. The father sees his son watching the television and sees the shows himself. He sees that the boy has come to know male heroes as static, one-dimensional men; Christ figures who save the baby from the burning building just in the nick of time, solve the brutal crime spree that has been terrorizing the town or win the big game with a walk-off home run in the ninth inning. Let's face it, children are shown a certain image of men over and over again. Men are warriors. Men are heroes. Men are rich, intelligent business people. Men are superstar athletes. This stereotype has changed very little in the last one hundred years. Just look at the soldiers spread across the evening news or Donald Trump's latest "reality show."

My father was a factory worker, or at least he worked in a factory. He was a commercial artist who designed lapel pins, hood ornaments and class rings that the factory where he spent his energy then manufactured. He hated his work and the people he worked with. He considered himself an artist whose talents were not appreciated and consequently wasted, working near an assembly line. From his drawing table he heard the droning *chung, chung, chung* of the assembly line throughout the day. Like many American men, he saw his work as a necessary evil. Also like many American men, he only told his son enough about it so that I would have the pieces of the propaganda puzzle to play with and combine with my television heroes, mythological figures and imagination to assemble together in his absence.

Perhaps, on occasion, the boy will go to the father's place of work. Perhaps it is "bring your kid to work day." In my case, my father's factory was located dramatically close to the minor league baseball stadium in our town. When we would go to games, my father would park the car behind the factory and we would walk down the street to the stadium. He would pull in behind the giant smelter smokestack and say, "That's what they use to melt the gold and silver. It can get up to ten thousand degrees. Then they pour the liquid gold into molds. If a man gets one drop of that on him—one tiny drop! —it will burn clean through his flesh and bone and come out the other side. I've seen it."

I would take these stories with me to the ball game and, when I got home, I would pile them inside the propaganda shop that was growing larger and larger in my house. Sometimes, on the weekends, I would ask my father about his war experiences and he would tell a short tale to dramatize his experiences. "I once saw a man get his head cut clean off by an airplane propeller," he would say. "He was a mechanic, and he left his wrench by the engine while the plane was starting up. He turned around to look and, wham!" I would take these stories with me back to the propaganda shop as well.

At some point the son stops playing in the propaganda shop and starts working there. He matures to a point where he can—he must— start imagining his own life as an adult man. He has the propaganda puzzle pieces to work with and he has the shards of his father's broken life in that room, too. After all, his father had certain dreams that were never realized.

My father had dreams of fighting the Japanese in the Pacific. As the story went, he received his order to ship out as a flight engineer in 1945. His next order of business was to propose to the teenage soda clerk he had been dating while stationed in Texas. After all, being a combat pilot over the Pacific was lonely as hell and did not carry with it a very good chance of returning alive. My future mother accepted, was nearly disowned by her family for her rashness and some sort of quickie ceremony took place, of which no photographs were taken. The young lovers had a few days together at the base hotel and then news bulletins came over the radio declaring an end to the battle in the Pacific. Or at least I imagine it to have been something like that. My parents never really talked about it.

On a dime, a life can turn. We all know people with such stories or we have experienced such dramatic changes ourselves. One day, my father was about to either become a war hero or die in combat; the next, he was an unemployed veteran with a pregnant, teenage wife and a pile full of youthful dreams that had to be tossed somewhere for safekeeping. He put them in the propaganda shop. Where else could they go?

So, as a boy, I had the crushed dreams and disappointments of a combat pilot, the frustrations of an unrecognized artist forced to be a tired factory worker and popular culture images to play with. My instincts told me to redeem the father who was lost to these forces. Like many boys do, I set about the task of rescuing my father.

The Father Mythology

By this time, the child has developed a sense that he has lost his father. He has seen enough of the world to know that the father mythology is an incomplete, if not wholly false, construct. His instinct to redeem his father is overwhelming. He must construct a father image and go beyond to construct an image of the man he himself wishes to become. The son begins by accepting, to some degree, the diminished idea of the father. He knows that some of his patriarch's life has been left at the factory, some has been tossed on the tarmac at the air base; there isn't much left. He takes what little he can scrape up and brings it into the propaganda shop and starts to arrange the pieces. But every time he starts to construct something resembling a whole, he finds he is missing pieces. It is a puzzle that has been hanging around the house too long and is now missing far too many pieces to successfully assemble. What can he do? He has no choice but to fashion the missing puzzle pieces from available materials.

Popular culture tosses hero images to male children at an alarming rate and with the shocking poignancy only adolescents can understand. It has always been this way. Former president Ronald Reagan and, before him, former president John F. Kennedy, are two examples. Both were wealthy, powerful, good-looking and popular. Reagan did not threaten men; men could appreciate his high morals and hold this idea out to their own families, even if they themselves were not up to the standard. Moreover, Reagan was willing to stand up to the Soviets, who were perceived in Reagan's time as a threat to American security, look them in the eye and have a full-blown staring contest on national television.

Like Reagan, John F. Kennedy was a leader. He was a war hero, but some felt he threatened American fathers with his good looks and the delicate beauty of his family. His assassination, however, placed him in a position for hero status. There were other hero figures, astronauts, businessmen like Ross Perot and T. Boone Pickens, media anchors like

Dan Rather and Walter Cronkite. Politics was a stronger force then than it is today.

So we took a little dab of Reagan, a smidgen of Kennedy and a pinch of some of the others who appeared on the cover of *Time Magazine* into my generation's propaganda shop. But we were still woefully deficient. We needed to bring out the big guns: television, music and sports. The pop culture triumvirate has never been short of role models for young males to draw from. During the 1980s and 1990s (and today), we had the Michael Jordans, Derek Jeters, Kurt Cobains and Tom Cruises to help fill the gap. We brought them into the propaganda room. And let us not forget the stories of Zeus and Apollo, King Arthur and Caesar, and the other mythological gods and kings we learned about in high school.

Having an absent father, a father who carries around with him a staggering disappointment, a codependent father, a substance-abusing father, a workaholic father—these all create injury in sons. The son takes with him those wounds and, at a certain age, often in the young teens, goes into the propaganda room with all of the puzzle pieces lying scattered on the floor and the popular culture heroes looming in the corners; he tries to put the puzzle together. His work is frustrating, mind-numbing and impossible. He follows a formula that looks something like this:

The mythological father (politics, pop-culture, mythology)
+
The imagined life of the father
=
The imagined life of the son

When he comes out of the propaganda room, usually in high school, the son thinks that he has determined who he is and what he is going to be. Really, he has just stumbled out of the jungle, malnourished, confused, sleep-deprived and sickly. He is lucky he has survived at all.

What he doesn't realize at this juncture is that in contrast to having all the answers, he is more confused than ever, and his own identity has never been further away.

The Weak and Strong Father

While the son is undertaking all this lonely work in the propaganda shop, the father is still around, trying harder than ever to control the situation. The son's adolescence brings with it an inevitable sense of discord and chaos. The father starts churning the propaganda gears. But by then the son has, at least in his mind, completed the work of assembling the puzzle. He isn't quite as open to the propaganda anymore.

In my own life, my father sought order in his life through screaming and psychological violence against his family. He had no control at the factory where he worked, but at home he tried to control the people around him with force, yelling and abuse. When he was calm, my father was filled with Teutonic thoroughness. He would sit at his desk for hours with a drafting pencil and ruler and create ledgers with hundreds of lines on which he recorded household expenses, car maintenance schedules, even lists of family birthdays. At his office, he might have sat under a magnifying glass for days, engraving a metal plate by hand with the corporate logo of some Midwest farmers' association. At work, his ability to concentrate and make order from chaos was incredible. But his pursuant fits and tantrums were legendary. His rages were otherworldly, sometimes lasting days on end when he would not sleep, only resting periodically in his room and then emerging to scream again for hours. He was a sick man, we knew. But since being committed to a veteran's hospital after a particularly violent episode involving a gun and a co-worker many years before, he had refused to see any doctor or therapist. He stayed off any potentially helpful medications, saved his fury for the home and managed to hold the factory job in a new town for over twenty years.

In contrast, weak fathers control their families through silent disappointment. They may build up expectations to an unachievable level, then dole out measured dissatisfaction to bring about the desired impact. Sometimes only a small facial gesture is needed. Other times, they may ignore the family or not speak to them for days. By the time adolescence arrives in the son, the father has lost the one thing that has stabilized his own identity: Control of the son. Fathers typically experience a crisis at this time in their lives. The door is open to a nervous breakdown, a midlife crisis, alcohol abuse and so on. Whatever name we apply, this period in a man's life is fraught with inevitable frustration and fear. The propaganda shop is now closed for business and two people's identities are at risk: the father's and the son's.

The presence of the propaganda shop and the absence of the father because of his economic obligations have changed the entire dimension of patriarchal identity—from both points of view, the father's and the son's. To refer again to David Brower's evolution metaphor, if the history of patriarchal relationships were a twenty-four-hour day, the changes we have seen, mainly because of industrialization—the most dramatic changes imaginable—have all taken place within the span of a few seconds of that day. Today, men are away from their sons the majority of their time because of work. The training and initiation of sons, therefore, no longer exists. Instead, the son is left with the dangerous remnants of male identity—the imagined life of the father, pop culture, mythological kings—and no instruction booklet to help him assemble the pieces. The propaganda shop opens its doors wide for male children, invites them in, but there is no guide, no ticket taker and no one to tell them what to do with the tremendous energy in that room. Without a guide and with such danger all around, it is no wonder so many males arrive at crises.

8

HEROES and
Role Models

One of the great benefits of a mythological belief system is the presence of heroic figures that show by example the way to adulthood. Men like Martin Luther King, Jr. and John F. Kennedy are two examples of such cultural heroes from the modern age. They inspired many young people in their era. At the time of what we now know to be their greatest triumphs, some in America despised them, or at least disagreed with them. It was only after their death that we came to recognize them as true heroes.

Today, adolescents rarely latch on to heroes whom they see as being too popular or too mainstream. Instead, they choose someone they perceive to be a nonconformist leader, although these are often media creations. History has its heroes as well, both real and mythological. Prometheus and Odysseus are two good examples from the Greek myths of heroes.

A hero, I believe, is someone who gives up personal gain for the greater good of society. This trait—selflessness—is a key ingredient in a hero. Much the same is the act of choosing to give up something for the greater benefit of others. Some have even said that the act of birth, both on the part of the mother and on the part of the baby, is the original act of heroism. The mother, we know, risks great tragedy during gestation and birth. The baby, on the other hand, forgoes the calm peacefulness of the amniotic sac for the uncertain future out in the world. Although the baby's transformation is not from choice (and in some cases neither is the mother's), the event provides the experience of heroism for both.

For a newborn who has thus tasted the experience of heroism, and therefore knows its meaning on an experiential level, the parent becomes the very first recognized hero. When the child is hungry, the parent brings the food. When there is a problem—the lights won't turn on, the car won't start or anything beyond the limits of childhood understanding—the parent fixes the problem. First it is the mother who shares in the initial birthing ritual and plays the role of hero to the child. But soon the father, if there is one present in the picture, takes on that dimension. The child knows that a hero must be willing to give their life for a greater cause or ideal. It is only recently that childbirth has become less of a mortal exercise. In the past, many mothers and babies died during childbirth. Many still do, especially in places around the world without proper medical care. In places like America, though, for many childbirth has become more a process, taking away the experience of mortality and heroism.

The other defining characteristic of a hero is the transformation from all to one. Heroes must give up their individual natures for communal natures, for ideologies based on communal good, in order to make the transformation. The shaman in tribal societies gives up not only his name, but also his role as father, brother, everything that defines him in order to serve the greater good of the tribe. The same can be said for the boy who goes to serve as a Buddhist monk in Thailand or the Catholic priest in Europe and America. These roles require a fundamental change in identity.

This transformation can be called atonement. It is based upon a principle of giving up one's individuality for a different identity, one beneficial to a group. Breaking the word down, we can see that it is at-one-ment: at one with the tribe, at one with the culture and no longer an individual. Identity acquisition in adolescence is at the root of the coming-of-age process. In pre-industrial times, identity was shaped through community influence. Today, media and popular culture play a much larger role in helping adolescents to shape their identities. Heroes who demonstrate atonement are still some of the best role models in a culture.

Adolescence is about making choices between continuity with the adult world as it is perceived and establishing personal uniqueness. American boys feel pressured to choose alignment early on in the coming-of-age process, and the pressure to establish individuality is equally powerful. Such exploration forms the foundations for lifelong belief systems and can either open the door to adulthood or shut it completely. In some cultures, the need for affiliation is deeply rooted. But in America we have, since the birth of our nation, placed a special emphasis on the individual. This is all well and good for adults who are emotionally and intellectually able to evaluate the consequences of their decisions. But for boys, feeling a pressure to become something, anything, and do so in a hurry, can be enormous and destructive. Absent are the coming-of-age practices that tribal cultures once supplied, and some boys easily turn to the most accessible sources for support in forming their identities. Popular culture provides an ample supply of skewed instruction on the matter, and the media has a now long-established competition for dominance in this area.

Most disturbingly, as Erik Erikson and other developmental psychologists have pointed out, adolescents often over-identify with heroes from popular culture sources such as television, music and movies. In the Elvis Presley era, tens of thousands of teenage boys wore sideburns and tight pants. What wasn't talked about at the time was their identification with the sexual experimentation and moral choices that went along with the media image they were pursuing. Often the outward symbols of identification are most easily recognized, but the inner personality choices are far more meaningful.

Erikson characterized the period of adolescent identification as a "crisis." Successful passage to adulthood and to achieving an integrated adult identity depends upon navigating the crisis successfully. His contemporary, J. E. Marcia, called those who made it through the process "identity achieved" and those who did not make it through successfully either "identity foreclosed" or "identity diffused." The "achieved" group, people who have confronted the identity formation process successfully, now represent a smaller and smaller portion of American adolescents. The members of the "foreclosed" group, whom Erikson says simply default to their parents' values and identity, represent a fair portion of the population, but have receded since the 1950s. The group that is affirming itself today, and expanding to epidemic proportions, is the "diffused" group, which is comprised of people who resist adult identities and are unable to make personal adult commitments to a career, family or set of values. They remain permanent adolescents, because they have not, or will not, address the identity crises life presented to them in their teenage years.

When one searches for a personal identity during adolescence, there is a powerful instinct that takes over. It is a loud voice that screams out to look to those who are living life the way the adolescent envisions it should be—as an artist, an athlete, a drummer in a rock and roll band. But as Joseph Chilton Pearce has said, the brain development that takes place in adolescence promotes an inherent idealism that comes to control that period of life. With idealism at its center, and a powerful yearning for independence and self-actualization, teenagers naturally seek mentors and role models for their development. It is the most important time in a person's life for identity development, and the influences that the boy comes into contact with during this time will shape the success or failure of the rest of his life. It is at this critical time that the educational system comes into focus in the teenager's life. With rigorous, standardized testing at its core, modern schools promote conformity and the belief that all boys must meet a single standard—in math, science, physical education, behavior and so on. I believe it is a philosophy that is directly opposite to the teenage boy's brain's inherent quest for individuality and idealism.

A Search for Identity

In the horizontal society, there seems to be a competition, more and more hostile in recent years, between the three functional parts of the brain. The new brain, for all of its idealistic potential for new development, seems fully occupied with attaining a more pervasive self, while the R-brain seems to prefer an entity with no self or, as some have said, many selves. The self identity as possessed by the new brain aspires an identity that is part of an economic order. That order is called consumerism and gives rise to most fields of science, which ultimately are in service to some form of consumerism in the economic order. Violence around the world is often directly related to this as well, whether it is street violence in Mogadishu between rival gangs battling for control of the gun and drug trade on a city block or the bombing of a village in Iraq where petroleum resources or sectarian dominance may be involved. It is the brain's resolute pursuit of the self that engenders these problems. The self we speak of, as constructed by most Americans, is an entity with economic considerations at its heart.

Once, a close friend of mine took a vacation to Thailand. Upon his return, I asked him if he had experienced anything interesting and he told me a story about visiting a Buddhist temple. He was staying in a medium-sized town and, wanting to visit a temple, he inquired about where to go. Several people told him that the most beautiful of the temples in the area was well up into the hills and had no roads leading to it, only footpaths. The next day he climbed and climbed up the trail to the temple, which took him much of the day. Finally, arriving at the temple tired and hungry, he peered in through the reed doors and saw the head monk dusting the floor of the meditation hall. He introduced himself and respectfully asked the monk if he might have a look around. The monk asked, "Why do you want to look?"

"I was hoping to receive a blessing," my friend answered, not quite sure how to respond.

"I'll be happy to give you a blessing," the kindly old monk replied, smiling, motioning to an offering tray on a table. My friend dug into his pockets and tossed a handful of baht onto the offering tray. Just as he began to turn back around, the monk struck him hard on the back of the head with his broom; the blow made a resounding *Whack!* My friend had been given his blessing.

Buddhists see the brain's need for an "I" as one of the fundamental causes of suffering. Anything that helps the brain clear itself of this line of thinking, or thinking at all, is a path back to the R-brain and back to the original consciousness that they term *nirvana*. Meditation, or *zazen*, is the preferred path to this realm, but the smack on the head, given that hours of meditation clearly did not stand in my friend's path, was the next best thing. Startling blows like this have been used for centuries by meditation teachers as a way to "smack the thoughts out of the heads" of their students. Being of original mind, or thoughtlessness, was the monk's most benevolent blessing. His method of teaching was to do anything necessary to smack the pragmatism out of his students' minds.

The Rastafarians and the Sufis both have a version of this idea as well, although theirs is accomplished through addition rather than subtraction. Rastafarians see themselves not as one entity, but as more than one, referring to themselves as "I and I." The latter "I" is thought of as their spiritual self and the former "I" as the physical self. From early in life they provide a work space for the spiritual side of the person. Some of the Sufi poets acknowledged the presence of the R-brain as well. Some, like the Persian poet, Rumi, spent their entire lives searching for its divine spiritual entity. Rumi, depending on the translation, sometimes calls this presence the "Secret One," "The Divine," "The Guest" or other such terms.

Ecstatic Love is an Ocean

Ecstatic love is an ocean, and the Milky Way is a flake of foam
*   floating on that ocean.*
The stars wheel around the North Pole, and ecstatic love, running in
*   a wheel, turns the stars.*
If there were no ecstatic love, the whole world around would stop.
Do you think that a piece of flint would change into a plant
*   otherwise?*
Grass agrees to die so that it can rise up and receive a little of the
*   animal's enthusiasm.*
And the animal soul, in turn, sacrifices itself. For what?
To help that wind, through one light waft
Of which Mary became with child. Without that wind,
All creatures on Earth would be stiff as a glacier,
Instead of being as they are,
Locustlike, searching night and day for green things, flying.
Every bit of dust climbs toward the Secret One like a sapling.
It climbs and says nothing; and that silence is a wild praise of the
*   Secret One.*

(Translation by Robert Bly)

Many tribal cultures use masks in their religious and ceremonial practices to acknowledge the "other self" and to allow a space for the second level of understanding. The Latin word for mask is "persona;" still today we use the term to describe that which is perceived by others but which may not be the essential truth of ourselves. Such traditions exist in cultures as distinct as the Hindus of India, the ancient Celts, the African bush tribes and the rainforest people of Malaysia. Again, we see the primary peoples developing a spiritual recognition of the "other self" throughout their mythology across giant geographical borders. It seems as though primal peoples have always seen the need for a work space for our contrived persona and a path back to the original mind.

The Buyya tribal people of India use wooden masks to connect with the god Kalyadev, from whom they seek help with agricultural needs. They perform their mask ceremony in a very particular way and on a specific and auspicious day each year. Two youthful, unmarried tribal members are chosen to wear the masks and ornaments and perform the ritual. Curiously, in the context of the ceremony, the youths are honored and worshipped, as opposed to being subjugated, and their unmarried status is seen as a powerful innocence, much like the coming of the spring growing season, which has its own power and a better chance of reaching Kalyadev in a favorable context. Wearing their adornments, the youths perform a ritual dance, sing and inquire about rainfall, harvests and hunting, building a frenzy in the village crowd that observes them. They appear to become possessed and transform from innocent children into something god-like, or monster-like. When the frenzy has reached its pitch, the villagers gather close in a circle around the two performers and the youths in the masks shout instructions to the group about when to plant, who should lead the hunting party and other important matters. The village believes these instructions to be straight from the deity's own mouth, and they act accordingly by following the instructions throughout the year.

This ritual tells us that in some cultures, the young are viewed as though they are a direct link to the gods. In our own culture, many of us view adults as the gods and children as the servants of the gods. By harnessing the mythological energy of children, the Buyya not only teach the young the importance of mythological practice, but also help substantiate a cultural norm that honors children instead of diminishing them.

⑨

Boys and
their Mothers

Modernity has served to divide many mothers and sons in both physical and psychic ways. In the past, the paternal culture diminished the role of mothers making boys into men. That job landed squarely on the father. But we know better now. A loving, attentive mother can help her son develop masculinity and provide a solid character foundation that is often lost in the disconnect between boys and their fathers, and boys and their culture. Most important, mothers have an opportunity to shape the emotional and sexual sides of their sons and to help their sons develop the character necessary to maintain successful adult relationships.

In the electronic culture, with true human connectedness so long abandoned, most men wear a mask constructed from their projected childhood dreams, their unrealistic and unattainable desires and the unrealistic media images of beauty, success and power that shower them night and day. Their masks help them to cover up all of the things the media culture tells them they should be but cannot obtain: Hollywood good looks, Wall Street wealth and instant respect and admiration. Few men can live up to these unrealistic expectations, and their feelings of loss can be overwhelming. Thus today's mothers and fathers construct an artificial world both for themselves and for their sons to see. The artificial world helps them to feel better about themselves, and they feel it will make their sons respect and emulate them. We fill the artificial world with television sets, computers, video games, cell phones, anything that might temporarily fill the guilt we feel because we are unable to properly parent or spend enough of our time and energy on our sons.

Mothers in the electronic culture have a unique type of shame and insecurity that is caused by the unrealistic expectations society has developed. Society expects working parents to provide economically and function professionally all day in the fiercely competitive workplace, but then return immediately to the nurturing role of a parent. Mothers, too, may find that their sons' instinctual independence is a threat when their attempts to nurture are rebuffed. We know that boys have an inborn instinct to be independent and to spurn a mother's emotional assistance.

Recently, researchers at Brigham Young University surveyed parents of unmarried college students ages eighteen to twenty-six, cites Patti Neighmond in her article "'Generation Next' in the Slow Lane to Adulthood." They asked one simple question: "Do you consider your child to be an adult?" Over 80 percent of the parents of these twenty-somethings said, "No, they are not yet adults." Clearly our expectations of adulthood have changed. In the mid 1950s and 1960s, Neighmond continues, the average age of marriage for men was twenty-two and younger for women; the majority of couples had their first child within a year of their wedding. Today, one-third of men and one-quarter of women never marry, and the average age of first childbirth has extended into the mid and late twenties as well. Our expectations have drama-tically changed in the past forty years. We no longer expect women to become mothers, and we no longer expect men to become fathers. We no longer expect our children to become responsible for themselves, and no one is much concerned with taking care of the world around them.

In recent generations—the present one included—too many boys have been left without the resources necessary to develop healthy emotional selves during adolescence. In part, this can be blamed on fathers who have abandoned their sons, either by leaving the family specifically or by abandoning the family de facto by choosing their careers as a priority. Indeed, the economics of modern life make that demand on many, if not most of us. So it is little wonder that mothers are left with more of the duties to help boys develop their emotional selves. But since the 1970s, mothers also entered the workplace en masse and became engrossed in the ways of American competitiveness.

Consider that in 1960 only about 38 percent of women age twenty and older were working, compared to over 60 percent today. So with a majority of American women in the workplace, we can conclude that the values of the American workplace are being taught to more mothers, who then bring them home to their sons. Values such as competitiveness, greed, consumption, shortsightedness and materialism have come to dominate American families, and it is no wonder we have lost the ability to teach empathy, compassion, respect and community to our boys. We should realize that economics have a far greater role in our children's lives than we have ever acknowledged. Schools teach our boys from a similar perspective. They study past culture's primitiveness; the starvation of the Jamestown Colony, the racism and inhumanity of the Civil War and the unfortunate days before the automobile. Instead of teaching boys to discover themselves and build new ways of living in the world, the school's mission is to reinforce the economic identity that is now established; the same one Mom and Dad come home with from the office.

A mother's love and support will make a boy stronger, not weaker. It is a myth to think that because women are more prone to emotional connectedness and talking things out that boys cannot relate to this type of learning and communication. Boys often develop language skills much later than girls. One consequence of this is that boys often react to emotional confusion in physical ways. Rob, a thirteen-year-old boy I taught, threw a basketball through his bedroom window. Later, when his mother and father sat him down to talk about the incident and ask Rob why he had done such a thing, he replied, "I was just so frustrated, you have no idea! I couldn't even yell, because I didn't know what to say." The lack of language development in boys has a very real consequence of letting aggression and intolerance take hold in their emotional regulation. Mothers have the best chance of breaking these cycles of aggression in boys.

Psychologist William Pollock notes that many mothers he sees want to raise boys who are sensitive, compassionate and responsive to their emotions and the feelings of girls. But at the same time, they want sons who are assertive, competitive and who won't be branded as "wimps" at school or beaten up on the playground. Society's expectations of boys often compete with an enlightened mother who wants her son to be both accepted and sensitive. The trick may be in encouraging both aspects of boys' personalities, while teaching them how to regulate and use each side of their consciousness. It can be a very difficult task.

Alex is an example. He was a ninth grade student whom I talked with extensively about his relationships with his mother and father and his struggles as an adolescent boy. "My mom wants me to be, like, sensitive with girls," he told me. "Understand their feelings; write them poems. Stuff like that." Alex's face sort of grimaced when he said these last words. "But my dad, he's like, 'Just go ask the best-looking girl out you can find! You're as good-looking as any kid in that school,' " Alex told me. "It's like he was saying, 'Just go out and take what you want,' you know?"

The confusion Alex was experiencing was coming from his parents' conflicting opinions about masculinity. Alex was hearing two opinions, and neither one created a profile that he felt he could obtain. He didn't see himself as a great lover or great looking. He lacked experience and confidence. So his father's advice to "just go out and get it" didn't feel quite right. But at the same time, his mother's assertion that he should try to connect to the emotional needs of teenage girls didn't feel comfortable either. I could see that with confusion like this, Alex was going to gravitate to the more available and easily accessible teachers on the subject: his peer group and the media.

I kept meeting with Alex and talking with him about his life, more to be a non-judgmental source to talk to than to be an advisor. That whole year Alex seemed to grow more and more confident in his masculinity—and I think his success in school sports and with one particular young lady who took the initiative with him had a lot to do with that—but I also noticed that he truly yearned for a more definitive relationship with his mother. She was the one he really talked to at home, and the one he really trusted. He admired his father and enjoyed spending time with him, but Alex also realized that he probably didn't have much insight when it came to girls. He trusted his mother's judgment on that subject. "She tells me what to get her [his girlfriend] for her birthday and, like, what to say to her on the phone and stuff," Alex confided to me. "God, if it wasn't for mom, Haley would have dumped me a long time ago."

Sometime around the onset of adolescence, mothers and sons may become disconnected. At this stage of development, boys seek independent male identities. They spurn the hugs and closeness that their mothers supplied in their childhoods. In turn, mothers feel shunned and rejected at their sons' new male identity formation. Mothers often react to this perceived rejection with a more assertive approach, trying to reach out more actively to their sons. He may be withdrawing to his bedroom and shutting the door, and she may be coming down the hall close behind, knocking, asking what is wrong. It is at this critical stage of identity formation that boys become susceptible to media and peer group influences as they seek their new domain. The door is now open to conflict and division in the mother-son relationship. The boy may be seeking a new identity—changing his hair color, experimenting with sex, alcohol, new types of music—but the mother has not adjusted. How could she? The changes in her son are so abrupt that it seems, at first glance, he has disavowed all of the love, attention and hard work that his mother has kept up for twelve or more years. The sense of rejection on both parts is remarkable.

It is important to keep in mind that in early adolescence, and throughout adolescence, however long that may last, mothers often hold the key to the emotional regulation of their sons. No matter how much conflict there may be over the practical matters of household life, teenage boys have a deep respect for their mothers' opinions. Like my former student, Alex, put it to me, "She's pretty much right about just about everything." Boys feel such a comfort level with their mothers, in fact, that they will often save their worst behavior, and their highest level of emotions, just for them.

It is easy for mothers and sons to fall into a downward spiral during the first few years of puberty. Deep down, boys need to legitimately perceive the approval and confidence of their mothers. But they are acting out; their hormones are running wild, their emotions are out of control and conflict is never far off. It is natural under these circumstances to disapprove of the choices that sons may be making. Mothers perceive a duty to challenge their sons if they are making mistakes. But in this challenge, boys will often perceive that they are receiving a "no confidence" vote from their mother, and the deep-set need to feel their mother's approval may be severed. In such cases, the boy's reaction can be debilitating.

Mason, one of my students, had a mother and father who kept close watch over him in high school as a ninth grader. His need for an independent identity had become undeniable, yet he pursued this need by falling in with a crew of rough boys who smoked, picked fights, disrespected teachers and did poorly in school. Naturally, Mason's mother was disturbed by her son's new choice of friends, and when Mason's grades began to slip, she decided to take a more assertive role. She called meetings with Mason's teachers and school officials to strategize, set strict limits on his behavior and did her best to enforce his limits. But I observed something else in Mason's reaction to his mother; I could tell that he had not changed his fundamental personality. He was still a good kid, but now that his mother was challenging him so assertively, he not only rebelled, but he also felt a deep sense of abandonment. Speaking with him about it privately, Mason told me, "If she can't back me up, then screw her. I'll just do whatever I want!" His behavior worsened, his poor choices deepened and by the end of ninth grade, Mason had dabbled in hard drugs, been suspended from school and failed three of five core courses.

Mason's case is not to say that his mother should have condoned his erratic behavior. However, few people ever fully realize adolescent boys' need to remain connected to and feel approval from their mothers. It is quite difficult for parents of either gender to feel supportive in the face of a culture of rebellion and cruelty in their own home. But the real key to success with boys of this age is to guide them and keep them safe, while still making them feel as though they are making their own choices and forming their own identities. Without feeling supported and connected to his mother, a pubescent son is in real danger of feeling abandoned and losing the stabilizing influence of his mother.

The innate connection between mothers and sons is one of nature's greatest accomplishments. Ancient art and clay figures portray mothers holding their infant sons to their left breast. It is a primordial physical connection, the first physical and psychic connection boys have in the world outside of the womb, and it is deeply metaphoric of their coming connectedness. Biologists know that cells can communicate even when they are physically separated in the laboratory and can synchronously develop in parallel. So, too, mothers will often comment on their physical, spiritual and psychic connection to their sons: "When he's outside without a jacket, I get cold," I heard one mother say at a dinner party.

This intuitive knowledge of their sons' needs is remarkable, and it is at the heart of the challenge mothers and sons face during coming-of-age. In our electronic culture, instead of encouraging the connection between mother and son, we have introduced institutional forces meant to separate son from mother and force boys to form artificial identities. Primary among the tools used for this purpose in the consumer culture are television, media and lifestyle marketing meant to grow consumer attitudes. Boys as a whole are feeling more and more abandoned. Whether it is a result of the physical disconnect begun in the hospital delivery room, the media messages they are bombarded with throughout their toddler years or the adolescent culture of violence and rebellion, we can only guess. But we know for certain that we are at war with our children in America. Rates of abuse have skyrocketed, with thousands of infants every year killed outright by their parents, and patterns of brutality, neglect and abandonment reaching epidemic proportions. An acquaintance of mine, an emergency room physician in New York City, commented that he sees close to a dozen kids in the emergency room each weekend, abused by their parents badly enough to need hospitalization. The rates of violence spread out like a spider web from childhood, and other chapters of this book discuss what becomes of an adolescent culture that reverts to violence as its primary means of communication.

Encouraging Emotional and Empathic Boys

As American critic and educator Neil Postman pointed out in the 1980s, our culture has "shriveled" to a point where there are only two models left: the Orwellian model, which is a prison, and the Huxleyan model, which is burlesque. In the new millennium, we seem to have combined the two, with varying elements of thought control interwoven or delivered as entertainment. But the underlying messages have been consolidated to the pragmatist ideals; creativity, the arts, spirituality, metaphysics and any mode of vertical development has become outcasted, banned or otherwise disavowed. Service to the economic ideal is omnipresent. Capitalist pragmatism reigns.

Postman said that in the electronic age, instead of Big Brother watching us and regulating us, we have been brainwashed into watching

Big Brother and willingly following his commands. It seems as though the brainwashing is now complete. We are taught to ignore everything except consumerism. In the past ten years, the United States has watched as genocide, ethnic cleansing, mass violence and severe human rights abuses have occurred in the Baltics, Darfur, Somalia, Congo, Tibet, China and elsewhere. Instead of intervening, we debated a little and ultimately ignored these atrocities. We have stood mesmerized by the latest movies and television comedies as global warming has begun melting the polar ice caps, killing the world's reefs and destroying the phytoplankton at the base of the food chain; we watch as desertification marches on, coastal buffer zones slide underwater, massive draught-induced wildfires rage across California and the West, even as once great American cities such as New Orleans are destroyed by floods and hurricanes. All of this while we refuse to take part in any meaningful agreements meant to reduce greenhouse gases. In the midst of this destruction outside our windows, we have elected pragmatist oil men to lead our government, and then followed them to war in oil-producing nations like Iraq and Afghanistan, sacrificing the lives of thousands of American soldiers and tens of thousands of foreign civilians, all while driving more than ever, buying more than ever and using more oil and coal than ever before. Our trance is so complete that the Orwellian spell Big Brother has cast is now beyond challenge. It seems like we are no longer able to even lift a finger to save ourselves, even as the bodies of our neighbors float by our window down our flooded streets.

We might say that the opposite of the Orwellian Big Brother phenomenon is a connection to the Great Mother or mythological mother goddess. While Big Brother's system is a type of prison created to control people's thoughts and behaviors, the Great Mother's system is the natural order of the world. The Great Mother is uninterrupted evolution, natural selection, the connection to the psyche's deep primal core and what we've previously called vertical development. She wants us to continue to develop without artificial restraints or controls, free of orchestration from corporate executives and media conglomerates.

The Great Mother has been given many names by many peoples who recognized her inherent value. Stone statues over 25,000-years-old showing *Mater Delorosa* (giver of life) or *Mater Natura* (natural mother) have been discovered, and primary peoples from all across the globe have founded their belief systems on the Great Mother's simple perfection. But she is more than an ancient archetype. She is the natural path to success and survival. As Carl Jung wrote: "Why risk saying too much…about…our mother, the accidental carrier of that great experience which includes myself and mankind, and indeed the whole of…nature?" Clearly Jung and his followers argued for a return to organic psychology and a connection to the deep psyche as a way of moving upward. The ways of primal peoples throughout history have already written a good deal of the book on how to connect to these primal places. In the context of modern male education, it is inexcusable to maintain that technology is a neutral force. We should recognize that coming-of-age in the traditional sense cannot be guided by a television set, yet that is exactly what teaches most boys today.

Forging a path away from the educational status quo is a difficult task, but may be the only way back toward *Mater Natura*. An inquiry-based educational system is a good first step. Boys are natural explorers, and education based around their own interests and their own choices will likely be much more palatable than education forced upon them. This concept is true both in the school building and in the home, as true for pre-teens as it is for older children. Inquiry-based education allows for student empowerment by letting boys' interests direct their education. Having a say in their educational path is a vital empowerment tool that builds a deep commitment to educational success.

We should take time to carefully consider the question of what constitutes good thinking and good education. For now, we are training our boys to become more like the stars of shows on television—soldiers, professional wrestlers, drug dealers, mafia types, even a serial killer like in the television show *Dexter* and other violent, competitive male figures who are held in such high esteem. But demystifying some of these male stereotypes may just be the first step in alluding to a way of life different than the one portrayed in the electronic culture's mirror.

When any hierarchy is dismantled—even if there is advanced planning, which is rarely the case—the initial result is a leveling chaos, where groups scramble to gain power and establish a role in the new organization. This process happens when governments fall, during corporate takeovers and in larger cultural phenomena, such as when the paternal culture in America fell, which happened over a prolonged period. Without any reliable hierarchy or paternal command to live up to, individuals are lost and group identities naturally dominate. It is as though since the fall of the paternal culture we have lived somewhat like the boys in William Golding's *Lord of the Flies*, on an island of half-adults, leaderless, struggling, viewing life as a game. As Golding himself once put it: "Man is born to sin. Set him free, and he will be a sinner, not Rousseau's 'noble savage.'" The boys lost on the island without any parents to show them the way are our sons in the present culture.

Part ③

Boys and Aggression

⑩

Is Violence
in Boys' Nature?

Violent, aggressive behavior in male adolescents is reported daily in the media and seen regularly on the streets, in schools and across society. Some psychologists have tried to explain the rise in male violence by suggesting that aggression is simply a trait of maleness; that perhaps the media is now paying more attention to acts of violence, especially covering attention-getting events like school shootings and gang murders. However, a closer look at many of today's adolescent boys shows that violence has become a defining cultural trait, an accepted rite and a replacement for the previous identity formation that was part of the pre-industrial culture.

While some have come to call youth violence a "national crisis," it is becoming a more and more accepted part of traditional culture. Whether it is observed during play among young boys on the school playground, bullying in the high school hallways or more overt acts of violent crime on the streets, there are few who have not been directly affected by the status of violence in our culture. Young boys are especially susceptible to becoming violent because of their acceptance of media messages and because of their genetic predisposition towards aggression. Most boys, however, do not understand the underlying cause of their aggressiveness, nor are they trained in the proper ways to handle it.

In this horizontal society, adolescent boys are embracing violence and are adopting violence as a common form of interpersonal communication. As reported by numerous measures, attitudes about violence are becoming favorable and behaviors involving teen violence are increasing on virtually all levels. The American Medical Association, for example, has reported that one in ten American boys has been kicked in the groin by the age of sixteen. Children are growing up being kicked, punched and pummeled by their peers as an everyday form of interaction. But that same acceptance of violence leads to greater acts of violence as it becomes ingrained in our daily consciousness. The firearms death rate for male teenagers more than doubled between 1985 and 1994. In the school hallways, teachers such as myself see acts of violence on an hourly basis. Boys pushing other boys as they walk down the hall; boys calling one another derogatory names like "fag" or "pussy." We see boys whose first reaction to a perceived insult is to become violent. We see shootings reported on the news every day committed by teenage boys over pocket money, girlfriend disputes or some random act of perceived disrespect. At the same time, we are seeing all over the culture an extension of this violence in the rising suicide rate among boys (the suicide rate among fifteen- to twenty-four-year-olds has more than tripled since the 1950s) as well as an increase in "danger sports," such as extreme skiing, motocross and skateboarding—activities that are far more likely to result in injury or death. It seems that many of today's boys not only feel bulletproof, but see violence and its extensions as acceptable, common forms of expression. Make no mistake: this is a change in the communal psyche of males in the horizontal society.

Aristotle remarked in the fourth century that a youth's turning point could be marked by the child's development of self-determination. The Greeks recognized that the quest for identity was a hallmark of what came to be known as adolescence. In her biography on anthropologist Margaret Mead, Mary Bowman-Kruhn writes that Mead, in observing the Samoan culture, noted that young adults, especially the young males of the culture, had little stress and turmoil while going through adolescence. She concluded that the Samoan culture's coming-of-age rituals, where kids were encouraged to watch traditional adult activities such as childbirth and sexual relations and to take part in important cultural work and tradition, provided them a safe transport to adulthood. She sternly contrasted this attitude with that which prevailed in the United States. She noted how deeply damaged many American teens were at the time (1920s) and how relatively peaceful and intact Samoan teens were.

Mead's findings were controversial, mainly because they were critical of how kids were being raised in America. However, her observations of the importance of myth and ritual in the lives of young adults are important. We see today that because our youth do not have a clear system for achieving a positive adult identity, cultural influences such as popular media have taken on the role of teacher and are teaching boys to accept violence as a way of life. Certainly Mead was correct when she related the failing nature of America's youth and the downward spiral that gained momentum and continues today. I believe the so-called "lost generation" of the 1920s endured, suffered the turmoil of World War II, endeavored an attempt at verticality in the 1960s and has now come to roost in the non-literate electronic age of the new millennium. Would anyone conclude that today's American children on whole are more successful than those in the 1920s?

Another disturbing consequence of the derailed system of adolescent development in America, in my opinion, is the disappearance of remorse. In my hometown, Rochester, New York, a typical northeastern, mid-sized city, about one in four teens lives below the poverty level—that's about fifty-five thousand children. According to J. David Hawkins et al in *Predictors of Youth Violence*, 31 percent of teens surveyed in 2000 said they had seen someone shot, stabbed or severely beaten in their neighborhood. 37 percent had witnessed the same at school. In 2001, the City of Rochester School District reported that there were 120 assaults in their elementary schools, and over one thousand suspensions for violence. The percentage of students who fail to graduate from the city's schools is close to 70 percent. Where I live there have been eleven brutal murders in the past months, crimes all committed by boys between the ages of fourteen and twenty-one. Recently, a young pregnant girl was killed when someone sprayed nine rounds from a handgun into the house where she was living. Apparently the trouble began when a group of girls, including the victim, passed another group of rival schoolgirls on the street. One of the girls cast a critical look at another, one side commented on it, another yelled, the groups dispersed and, later that night, a boy affiliated with one of the gangs fired on the rival's house. After the shooter was arrested, he commented to the media at his hearing, "What did you expect me to do? They dissed me!" He showed no remorse throughout his hearings and barely any at his sentencing on murder charges that put him behind bars for twenty-five years, where he joined the growing legions of African-American young men.

In another telling incident in my hometown, a group of high school age boys got into an argument with Dana, a seventeen-year-old, at a Saturday night house party. Dana and another boy were interested in the same girl; they shoved each other and, outnumbered, Dana left the party and drove off. But the other boys weren't finished. They piled into cars of their own, two carloads filled with seven teenagers, caught up with Dana, forced his car off the road and pushed him to the ground. Amid what witnesses later described as Dana's "whimpering and pleading for mercy," two of the young men stabbed Dana thirteen times with a six-inch long hunting knife while the others watched and cheered. These were, by all accounts, typical teenagers having a typical teenage dispute. The difference, however, is the murder that took place over a minor incident. It is an example of the growing trend of seeing life as irrelevant and violence as ordinary in the teenage worldview.

These episodes are not unusual, neither in their frequency nor in their depravity. What has come to characterize teenage bickering in twenty-first century America is deadly violence and a complete lack of remorse. As a teacher, I routinely catch kids pushing, shoving, bullying or calling names. This is not unusual, but the attitude of the kids has taken on a new dimension. When a teacher calls attention to their actions, today's boys are no longer repentant. They stare back at the adult with complete defiance in their eyes. "What are you going to do about it?" they say. Television and electronic media teaches children that aggression is beneficial. Movies like *Scarface* and *The Godfather* have replaced real adult role models. Guns have become as common as baseballs to many American boys. Many have friends who have died of violence, and some have participated in the retributions that continue the cycle of violence. I hear children in school all the time discussing the merits of a Tech-9 assault pistol over the ever-popular Glock 9mm. Real violence has replaced the competition on the baseball and football field that once dominated in American culture. Today some boys are shooting one another rather than proving their worth on the playground or the ball field.

I believe our culture no longer maintains a moral center and youth are inheriting and increasing the cyclical lack of remorse and lack of shame that our culture now propagates (it is interesting, as well, that we do not have a sufficient word in the English language for this lack of shame, perhaps because the phenomenon is so new). But specifically, the absence of male nurturing and the routines and rituals of coming-of-age have left the landscape empty and popular culture has moved in to teach children how to perceive violence, how to respond to threats and how to interact with the world—skills that were once taught by the family system in the days of the paternal culture. Too many boys are now alone in their adolescence. The absence of a guide, or better, a culture to help guide them, results in many of the problems adolescents experience today.

The Roots of Male Violence

Research indicates men have an internal predisposition to violence. Through our ancient mammalian genes, men inherit violent tendencies, or at least an internal mechanism that lets violence creep into their temperament. But it goes much deeper than that. Our culture puts a tremendous amount of shame on men, and men do not know how or do not have the proper mechanisms to deal with their shame. Male children are especially prone to being shamed as they grow older and can be especially shamed by their fathers. So young men are growing up not being expressive, not knowing how to express their anger in positive, or at least in nonviolent, ways. I feel the nonviolent movement under Dr. Martin Luther King, Jr. in the 1960s never successfully addressed the roots of male anger in the black or white communities.

Adult men do not feel safe expressing their nonviolent sides, and younger men in a horizontal society never learn how to address it. Society tells them that it is okay to be violent as a means of expression—they watch football and professional wrestling, and television sends a message that it is correct to act on their internal feelings of aggression. But we know that this message can be quite dangerous and damaging. Male expressiveness is stomped out all over the horizontal society. In the work-place, individuality is pushed down in favor of the corporate identity. In the schools, the peer group identity is far more powerful than the personal identity. So men have a void; a void that develops in adolescence and expands after high school, and television is always present to fill that void, especially during adolescence when the window for personal identity formation is wide open.

Often, the alcohol and drugs that so many teenage boys come into contact with are really just tools to help them numb themselves from the shame they feel for not being able to express themselves or for not being able to understand or accept their true identity. Their identity may be something as complicated as that of a homosexual boy in an unsupportive household or school or as simple as an unfit boy in an environment dominated by athletes. Body image, while a common issue for girls, is also a widespread issue for boys, but is rarely talked about. All of these issues are repressed in the horizontal society and the message teenage boys hear is to not express these problems. Thus shame is allowed in, and boys who feel shame are apt to become violent or aggressive.

In our culture, I believe we have two problems: the inherent aggression that is built into males as an evolutionary trait, and the frustration and shame that is built up in men because they have not been able to express their aggression or true identity over the course of their childhood or adolescence. In the old culture there was an outlet. In the past, myths and stories allowed men to express their frustration and thus expel their anger. The gods and heroes in the stories did this for them. But our culture has abandoned its stories, and I have come to feel, because of my research and teaching experience, that we have tens of thousands of men and boys walking around with boiling anger inside them, an anger about to spill over in dangerous ways, at their co-workers or bosses, at their spouses, at their classmates. It shows up in our divorce rates, in our incarceration rates, in our failed families. We should think of how many relationships could be saved if men could express their thoughts and feelings—specifically their aggression—without anger or violence. Women tell men to do this all the time, but women have always had the ability to do this better than men. Men have never been able to do it well, and there has never been a cultural mechanism for safe male expression in the horizontal society.

Television, movies and pop culture have become the lead teachers for male children in our society. Violence is the key to success for most television shows and movies. Pop culture heroes like Arnold Schwarzenegger, Russell Crowe and Mel Gibson are teaching children that expressing violence out of frustration or for personal gain is correct. Hip-hop culture and its plethora of male heroes who espouse violence teach kids the same thing. The old lessons were about mitigation, reservation, regulation of emotion, intervention and moderation. The new lessons are about kicking butt and asking questions later. Today, boys in school have been trained that if others make them mad, hit first and discuss it later. I hear kids in the school hallways all day long threatening and bullying one another, even threatening their teachers and parents. I've had fifteen-year-olds threaten to punch me in the face because I asked them to stop talking in the classroom, and I have seen teenage boys attack their fathers in the school foyer, spilling blood on the floor.

Part of the vacancy that affects young men is a lack of responsible elders in the home, but also in political and popular culture. Children look to their immediate family for role models; however, the power and prestige of cultural heroes should not be discounted. The male role models in our society have taken on a set of diminishing moral and spiritual traits in a progressive way since the 1960s. Even those who have been seen as cultural superheroes, men like John F. Kennedy and Martin Luther King, Jr., have had their infidelities and/or less admirable aspects of their lives portrayed in the media. More recently, men such as former president Bill Clinton, actor/comedian Bill Cosby and former New York Governor Eliot Spitzer have also had less admirable moments in their private lives spotlighted in the press. Where should a young man look for guidance? Professional athletes? Politicians? Movie stars? This is a perplexing question.

There are too few positive role models. They have been eliminated from our culture due to the system of rewards and consequences of becoming one. If we think about it, we see that our culture rewards men for becoming anything but a role model. The gangster rapper with the longest arrest record and filthiest language often is the one making millions of dollars from the T-shirts emblazoned with his face that are worn by twelve- and thirteen-year-old boys around the country. The professional athlete who chokes his coach or gets caught with drugs often wins the giant contract. All around us, we see examples of horizontal thinkers reaping huge rewards for becoming the wrong kind of role models.

But where are the right kinds of role models? What are their rewards? We all know effective teachers, social workers, nurses and others. They work endless hours, are paid some of the lowest relative wages and are generally looked down upon by society. This indicates why our kids are growing up to not only think horizontally, but are also aspiring to be anything but a "helper."

Violence in the Schools

March 22, 2005, was another in a long string of cold, snowy days in Minnesota's northern plains. That morning, seventeen-year-old Jeff Wiese, a student at Red Lakes High School who had been on suspension for several months, killed his grandfather and his grandfather's girlfriend. Then he took his grandfather's guns and car, drove to the school where he entered through a metal detector, shot a security guard and a teacher, then proceeded to kill three other students, wound seven more, and finally kill himself in a classroom as police closed in.

The Red Lakes incident was the second school shooting in Minnesota in eighteen months. A shooting at Rocori High School had previously killed two students. Newspapers today are filled with articles about teenagers who have either planned or committed horrible acts of mass violence in their schools. Just as recently, in Riverton, Kansas, five teenage boys were accused of planning a shooting rampage in their school on the anniversary of the Columbine massacre. According to authorities, there have been at least ten cases in the last year where police were able to foil planned school attacks by students. The 2007 Virginia Tech massacre was a stunning reminder that not all of the violent plots are caught in time. In 2008, the shootings and deaths at Northern Illinois University were another grim sign.

These incidents constitute a pattern of compassionless adolescent boys. Within a year and a half of the Columbine incident, for example, American schools endured a dozen other shootings and countless other acts of violence. According to the United States Department of Education and Justice, in 2003, one in twenty children was a victim of some form of theft or violent crime at school. Ironically, the department's report on the matter went on to express its pleasure with this figure and its confidence that youth violence and delinquency had "leveled off." These figures indicate that there were about 787,000 individual acts of reported violence against children committed by other children in schools in 2003. Teachers were victimized by violent students sixty-three thousand times that year.

It is not the frequency of violent crime in schools and on the streets that is the only concern. Some measurable rates of violent crime among teens have actually declined during the past ten years. I worked in a school where fistfights were common and students who carried knives and even guns was a somewhat regular occurrence. But many teachers who have been around a long time say that it is nothing like it was in past decades. School violence, they assure me, was once a daily phenomenon. "At least we go days or even weeks without a fight now," one teacher told me recently. Most concerning is the change in attitude among teenagers in recent years. Most have lost any measure of empathy or compassion. I sometimes bring in stories from the newspaper about teen-related tragedies and ask the kids in my classes to read and discuss these current events in their community. Most are bored beyond description at having to read about yet another murder/suicide or school shooting rampage. Some begin closing their eyes or hiding behind their sweatshirt hoods. A few even begin cackling and laughing when they hear the stories. Violence is as normal as breathing to today's children and nothing is shocking any longer.

David Walsh is a psychologist and media researcher in Minneapolis, Minnesota. Commenting on the school shooting in nearby Red Lakes, Walsh said that television may be at least partially to blame for "rewiring" kids' brains and implanting violent scripts that are then followed in real life. Speaking to Dan Olson of Minnesota Public Radio after the Red Lakes shooting, Walsh said, "We can't blame all of this on the culture and the media. But it's part of the combination of emotionally unstable kids—very, very angry, often bullied by other kids—who then fantasize, and the fantasy about violence and retaliation gets reinforced to the point that it reaches this tragic conclusion." Others, such as Michael Gurian in his book *The Minds of Boys*, have commented that the teenage mind has become so used to instant gratification through television watching that the use of firearms has become a perfect fit for their violent or unstable tendencies. With the availability of guns—both legal and illegal—being quite substantial, the child's mind searches for the instant gratification for which it has become accustomed through years of television viewing and playing violent video games. When their impulse is anger or revenge and guns are within arm's reach, there is clearly the potential for violent disaster. We, too, cannot discount the impact that watching on average two-hundred thousand acts of violence on television and in video games and thirty-three thousand murders, all by the age of sixteen, is having on our children.

The normalization of violence on television and in video games popular with teenagers is a major factor in the change in attitude and the increasingly violent nature of adolescent culture. The video game industry, for example, is a 25 billion dollar a year behemoth that has tremendous political and social influence over what kids see and do. The industry's primary motivation has been monetary, and it has only been recent that any serious attention has begun to have been paid to the effect such programming has on children. We have an economic history in this country which we might call *Fire, Ready, Aim!* We develop and sell new technologies, engrain them into our daily culture if they are successful and make a profit and then, after it is much too late to mitigate them, investigate their negative effects. We have seen this process unveil itself over and over again in products such as PCB compounds, which were used in electrical transmission but were shown to be poisoning us through the food chain. The same occurred in the case of the chemical DDT, which along with its use as a crop pesticide was sprinkled over the bodies of sleeping infants and toddlers to keep mosquitoes and lice away. It wasn't until Rachel Carson's *Silent Spring* alerted us to the danger that we reconsidered its use. There are a thousand other examples, ranging from drugs like Thalidomide to popular painkillers, that may either kill us or injure us. Some of the threats of these products and technologies are easier to understand than others, and many are very difficult to remove from the product stream once they have become ensconced in our daily lives. Television, video games and other electronic media should be considered in much the same way as we once looked at DDT, painkillers or any of the other products which at first seemed harmless, even helpful, but later were shown to be deadly.

As Dr. Christakis and others have pointed out, electronic media and its "passive, hypermechanical stimulation" not only encourages disorders like ADD in children, but also hinders brain development on both a neuronal, developmental and genetic level. The content of electronic media is a particular concern, but so is the very medium itself.

Studies by many respectable researchers, such as Vincent P. Mathews of the University Of Indiana Medical School Of Medicine, show that kids who play violent video games have brains that tend to "misfire" and have slowed brain activity. They are prone to develop a condition called "Disruptive Behavior Disorder." Mathews studied what he calls "heavy users," or kids who play several hours of video games per day. Dr. Carol Rumach of the University of Colorado added that the children had become so desensitized that they could no longer, "Understand the real effects of violence."

Several longitudinal studies have been conducted that demonstrate that children who play violent video games, watch violent action films and visit internet sites that promote violence become more violent themselves. In a report by the National Institute on Media and the Family, David Walsh et al. studied over four hundred fourth, fifth and sixth grade children who were rated on their aggressiveness towards peers, teachers and family over the course of a year. All of the children in the study were considered to be average or above average watchers of media violence. A major trend was identified in the children. Their level of aggressiveness clearly increased over the course of the year. Children who once sat down when the teacher asked them to were now shouting back across the room at the instructor. Kids who once walked away from verbal disputes on the playground slapped their rivals across their faces. The children's behavior was both self-rated and rated by on-the-scene observers.

The researchers expected to see a trend towards aggressiveness in their subjects. But they also found out something unexpected: the children who watched a lot of violence in the media were becoming antisocial. They began to shy away from peer interaction. They played less with their friends, declined to take phone calls and were observed sulking alone during free time on the playground. It is possible that the normalization of violence that our children are experiencing has shaped their worldview in such a way that they not only no longer trust adults, but also lack empathy for their own peers. We see the "adult" version of these ten-year-olds now; they live their life without a romantic partner, have difficulty holding a job and cannot relate to others in a normal way. Their emotions are stunted, their compassion lost to a world they know to be ruled by heartless bank robbers, machine-gun wielding gangsters and random drive-by shootings, all of which played themselves out throughout the fabric of their childhood across television screens and computer monitors.

In the United States, homicide and suicide account for about one-quarter of the deaths of persons ages ten to twenty-four. According to the Center for Disease Control, 12.8 percent of high school age children get into some sort of physical altercation at school each year, and on any given day 6.1 percent of students are armed with some type of weapon.

In their 2001 report titled "School Health Guidelines to Prevent Unintentional Injuries and Violence," the CDC notes that, "approximately 20 percent of female high school students have reported being physically or sexually abused by a dating partner" and "25 percent of male and female students in eighth and ninth grade have been victims of nonsexual dating violence." We can see from the figures that violence, and particularly violence of a sexual nature, contrary to the media's assertion that youth violence has diminished, is actually at staggering levels. Much of the misconception that youth violence has decreased is due to the comparison data that associate present levels with levels from the 1980s and early 1990s when the nation's crack epidemic was at its all-time peak. However, comparing present levels and attitudes of youth towards violence and suicide to the same levels and attitudes of previous generations gives a much more realistic picture.

Adolescence has always been associated with extreme emotions. But at present 19 percent of kids under the age of eighteen have suicidal thoughts each year and 15 percent go so far as to make specific plans for ending their lives. We are in the midst of a generation of teens who do not know how to effectively regulate or deal with their emotions. I see many children in eighth, ninth and tenth grades who threaten suicide over incidents such as being teased for new hairstyles, anger at boyfriends or girlfriends who talk to members of the opposite sex or non-chemical depression stemming from any number of what are typically considered to be minor teenage setbacks. Some of these children cut themselves or attempt suicide. Sometimes, one succeeds. It seems to me one major difference has become that today's children do not go to parents or other trusted adults to help them work through their emotional struggles; instead, they bury their feelings inside, take cues from the media and popular culture about how to react and then respond with violence, either upon themselves, their romantic partners or their peers.

Darrin, one of my students, was an eleventh grader, good looking, athletic and an excellent student. He was the kind of kid that every teacher dreams of: he answered questions readily in the classroom, behaved himself in the hallways and had his mind focused on social issues and causes, rather than the mundane topics most adolescent boys find themselves fascinated with. During parent conferences, his mother and father came to school, demonstrated their support of Darrin and asked to be contacted by teachers if there was anything going on that they might need to help with. There never was. Darrin gave no signs of being depressed and never raised concerns in his teachers or counselors. They often made positive comments on his report cards. But Darrin, like many adolescents, was socially withdrawn. Although he played on the school's baseball team, he didn't seem to have a lot of friends and was often seen walking the hallways alone. He didn't have a girlfriend and didn't go to the school dances. Just prior to midterm exams, Darrin came to see me for extra help. We spent an hour going over the material that would be on the test, and Darrin admitted that he was nervous about his midterms, but smiled. I tried to comfort him by telling him that I was sure he would do just fine. There was nothing to suggest that Darrin was thinking suicidal thoughts during that meeting; his demeanor seemed a little off, a bit more distant than usual. But that was Darrin. He didn't give a lot of information and mostly stuck to business when with his teachers.

The next morning, the day before midterm exams, as the class mingled and chatted in homeroom, the principal came on the loud speaker to make the announcement that Darrin had committed suicide the night before and that anyone who needed to speak with the counselors could do so that day. The principal said he was very sorry for all of us who knew Darrin and that the school had lost a good student and fine young man. We observed a moment of silence in Darrin's memory.

Darrin's case, to me, was an example of one prominent attitude of some of today's adolescents: independence, isolation and resignation. These traits are learned traits. Darrin clearly lacked a support system to which he could turn when whatever demons were tormenting him crept into prominence and took over his life. Darrin mistrusted the teachers in his life, likely even myself, though at the time it seemed as though we had a good, solid, teacher-student rapport. Little did I—or any of his teachers—know the levels of despair he felt.

①①

Blood, Gore
and Young Males

Today's adolescent culture is embracing resignation and destruction. There are no clearer symbols of this than the current fixation with death in popular culture. The top rated network television shows in 2006 among young adults was the *CSI (Crime Scene Investigator)* franchise. Similar programs like "Forensic Files" and "Real Stories of the FBI" have dominated the airwaves in recent years. Even whole networks such as Tru TV (formerly Court TV) have sprung up to accommodate the adolescent celebration of crime and death. Kids, especially boys, revel in the blood and gore of death scene investigation. They rush to school so they can discuss last night's episode in the hallways: "Did you see that guy's arm torn off and lying in the parking lot?" they ask each other excitedly. "It was sooo cool!"

According to David Bauder of the Associated Press, during one week in September 2005, there were sixty-three dead bodies visible during prime time television shows on six broadcast networks. Teenage channel surfers during the eight to ten P.M. time slot viewed the lead character in Fox's forensics drama, *Bones*, discovering a decomposing body hanging from a tree with crows picking at the human remains. The maggot-covered head of the corpse fell off and landed in the lead character's hands. Viewers of television that week also caught a gunshot victim screaming while blood spurted from a gaping chest wound, a car crash victim bouncing off a taxi cab's windshield and a suicide diving off an office tower and landing in a bloody heap on the street below. Television network executives openly admit to increasing the gore factor to gain audience share. "I think one of the drawing cards of *CSI* is that it is depicted very real and sort of gross," said David Janollari, Warner Brothers entertainment president. "It's part of why the audience comes to see it."

"Gore is not a goal in and of itself," says Peter Liguori, Fox Entertainment president, in an *Associated Press* article by David Bauder. He claims that television has had no choice but to increase the level of violence and gore in order to compete with movies and cable television, which increased the shock factor long ago. Each of these media channels, much like the children's cartoon suppliers, has noticed that they must up the number of startle effects in their programming in order to retain viewers who are becoming increasingly numb to the traditional sex and violence that once caught audiences' attentions. But even Liguori, who has children ages eleven and fourteen, said he knows *CSI* is not appropriate for most kids. But he said it's up to parents to monitor and decide what their children should watch.

During the 1990s there was a sizeable outcry from the American public when they felt too much violence pervaded the public airways and began negatively affecting children. Two groups that headed the opposition to television violence in the 1990s, The National Coalition on Television Violence and the National Alliance for Non-Violent Programming, have both waned due to lack of support in recent years. Much American culture seems to have accepted media violence as a given. The main focus of media complaints now comes from conservative groups and individuals complaining about the media's liberal attitude toward televised sexuality and profanity. It seems ironic that the Federal Communications Commission has levied millions of dollars in fines for network indiscretion such as Janet Jackson's infamous breast-bearing

Super Bowl performance, while at the same time staying silent as dozens of graphic murders are shown on prime time television programs weekly.

Smith and Donnerstein conducted a three-year study in 1998 of violence on television. They found that a majority of television programs (63 percent) contained some form of violence. Often, perpetrators of the violence were portrayed as attractive and successful and rarely faced any meaningful consequences for their actions. The negative consequences of television violence are well documented. Since 1950, there have been over one thousand studies on the effects of television violence on young viewers. According to a 1999 Senate Subcommittee hearing, children who watch violence on television are more aggressive and are much more likely to commit acts of violence than children who do not watch such programming.

Even with mountains of evidence arguing against violent media programming, mainstream academia has also jumped on the death bandwagon. Pennsylvania State University, for example, recently developed Bachelor's and Master's degree programs in forensic sciences and crime scene investigation, which sprang mainly from the demand generated by the popularity of *CSI* and related television shows. Some high school science courses are now using crime scene investigation techniques to teach students how to use laboratory equipment and are even taking students as young as fourteen to the local medical examiner's office on field trips where they are able to view dead bodies and autopsy dissections in progress. We are seeing a culture conform to new norms of acceptance of violence and a nonchalance about life and death. The normalization of violence also may cause children to grow up thinking that violence is the constant state of interpersonal interaction.

Video games aimed at teenage boys are another example of the electronic culture's fixation on death. *God of War, SoCom II, Call of Duty, Medal of Honor, Golden Eye, Desert Storm* and other PlayStation and X-box games mimic the death and violence of the military battlefield. One middle school student told me, "It's just like killing somebody, only better!" In games such as *Grand Theft Auto,* points are awarded for killing people, stealing cars and robbing stores, and dollars are awarded for murdering innocent people walking down the street. Characters in the game carry terrorist style weapons such as C4 explosives, AK-47 assault rifles and handguns. A skillful player might "kill" over one hundred innocent civilians. The best thing about the game, another teen told me, is that there aren't any real consequences.

According to Huston, et al, 1992, by the time a child reaches his or her eighteenth birthday, they will have witnessed two-hundred thousand acts of violence on television and video games and over forty thousand murders. The constant barrage of violence affects the developing brain in its capacity to interpret, react to and generate appropriate emotions in response to violence. A child who sees killing after killing throughout his or her life will develop a far different attitude about violence than will a child who has not had such normalization.

Recently, an art exhibition at the South Street Seaport in New York offered an exhibition called "Bodies...the Exhibition." The show featured the preserved corpses of twenty-two people and 260 "other specimens, including a set of conjoined fetuses, a set of male genitals, a pudgy woman who has been vertically sliced into four segments and a sprinter whose flayed muscles fly around him like slices of prosciutto," as phrased by *New York Times* reporter Andrew Jacobs in his review of the show in the newspaper. The sponsors of the show charged admission of $24.50 for adults and $18.50 for children and expected to make back their twenty-five million dollar investment during the installation's six-month run—much of it from youth groups, to whom they specifically marketed their exhibit. The blatant celebration of death and the use of cadavers as art and entertainment is another in the long and growing list of culture's celebration of death, commemoration of the end of vertical thinking and resolution to accept and live within a world dominated by the aftermath of the extermination of psychic growth. Our perspective on death seems to have come about with a certain indifference that diminishes the virtue of life. It is not only inconsistent, but also impossible to teach children the importance of preserving and respecting life while at the same time displaying flayed corpses for amusement on their field trips and splattered bodies on the sidewalks as their evening television and video game entertainment. Previously, we might have said they were receiving a mixed and confusing message about the adult world's attitude about life; but today, the message is far more weighted towards a disrespect for life in all of its forms. A culture that devalues individual life is more prone to violence and suicide, but also more prone to environmental destruction, dissolution of families and mistreatment of its poor, its disabled and its children.

The colonial impulse has coupled with the fascination with death and murder, because it has become institutionalized. In my opinion, that mindset has resulted in the present wars in Iraq and Afghanistan and elsewhere. Even the leadership of the United States has gone so far as to call these wars *ideological* in nature. I feel President George W. Bush essentially said that we are killing thousands of foreign young men (and many domestic) over a difference in belief systems. To me, his statements imparted a clear Judeo-Christian mentality, a colonialist mentality that requires direct, violent confrontation of other belief systems, including beliefs in psychic growth and vertical thinking.

Part of the danger of the colonialist progression is that the conquistador's attitude has turned inward and is now revealing itself in a backlash against adolescence. We are seeing in more and more American cities, and around the Western world, adults committing violence against adolescents; teens throughout the Muslim world are being adopted into the Hajj and martyr brigades in Iraq, Somalia, the Palestinian Homelands and elsewhere, as they are now seen to be a reliable and malleable first course in a murderous buffet.

As William Raspberry in the *Washington Post* and many others have documented, this backlash against adolescents has hit the African-American community very hard. Raspberry and other commentators have written furious columns about comments former White House Education Secretary William Bennett made. Bennett said, "You could abort every black baby in this country, and your crime rate would go down." Of course, relating his words doesn't provide a context, but even in the best interpretation his attitude reflects a growing sentiment in American politics: African-American teenagers are a menace and should be fought. Bennett went so far as to say *aborted*.

The leaders of the nation are not alone in their fear of male teenagers. We all see the crimes being committed. The murders and fights; the gangs and drug sales on the street corners. Those of us who work in public education see the daily harassment, bullying, defiance and disrespect that boys so readily exhibit. Those of us who have been in the education world long enough will tell you that these behaviors are not new, but are increasingly widespread.

Also, we are now seeing too many of the current adolescent generation of boys turn their violence toward each other. As I mentioned earlier, I live in by what in most accounts is a very average, midsized eastern city. The local newspaper dedicated its entire front page to the dominant story of recent months: teen street violence that has resulted in the deaths of numerous kids under eighteen in the preceding weeks. But these kids were unusual, even among the tragedies that are always present when a teenager dies. Almost all of the kids who recently died on my streets were killed by other adolescent boys.

One untimely death was a kid named Stacy "Bam" Long, a fifteen-year-old who attended the middle school where I once worked as a teacher. It is located in a poor and difficult neighborhood in the inner city. Bam was thought to be one of the kids who was ambitious and a good student. He was working his way out of a challenging situation. One Thursday night, Bam prepared to leave the house he shared with his mother. She told her son she was worried, because there had been so many young people gunned down in their area lately. Later, she told the local newspaper that Bam assured her he was not involved in anything criminal, that he would be all right. "Mommy, I won't be doing nothing to be killed over," were reportedly his last words to her. About an hour later, Bam was walking through the lot of a neighborhood recreation center where he was a regular. Someone shot him several times with a handgun. The article stated that police suspect Bam's murder had something to do with previous killings in the neighborhood; that perhaps Bam had been a witness to something in the past and was killed over fear that he would talk to the police.

In an additional incident during the preceding weekend, Devon Scott, a fourteen-year-old African-American, was stabbed to death outside a bar in a different neighborhood. Apparently, Devon was walking home when he came across some altercation of which he was not part. Devon, like Stacy Long, was known to be a kid who was not into drugs or gangs, but rather sports and positive activities.

Both of these deaths, and those of the other youngsters who were killed on my city's streets, prompted local officials to try and find solutions to this debacle. The police commissioner called for a conflict resolution curriculum in the schools; the school superintendent supported this and teamed up with the mayor to request over a million dollars in extra funds to add programs, staff, extra police and counseling to help ease the growing violence. But nothing has changed.

Elephants

National commentators like William Raspberry, who are noting similar nationwide trends in youth-on-youth violence, called for other relief as well. His ideas, while falling far short, were a little more realistic than those of Rochester's politicians. Raspberry related the story of adolescent elephants in South Africa's Pilanesberg Game Park. The elephants had been relocated to Pilanesberg some years earlier from Kruger National Park in an effort to relieve population pressures. The problem began when the transplanted elephants, about a dozen years later and now dealing with adolescence, began showing violent and antisocial behavior. In particular, they began harassing and attacking one of the park's endangered species, the white rhinoceros. They were chasing the rhinoceroses, attacking them with sticks held fast in their trunks and trampling many to death. Park managers were perplexed. There was plenty of food and little environmental pressure to inspire such uncharacteristic behavior.

In a desperate move, park managers decided to try a radical idea. They transported into Pilanesberg several adult male elephants from Kruger Park. They hoped that the presence of role models would serve to teach the adolescent males how to properly behave. It was their last attempt at a solution before killing off the young males. The park managers were delighted to find that the plan worked. The larger adult males quickly assumed a place of leadership in the herd, took over the partnering roles with the females and intimidated the younger males into relinquishing their violent ways. The white rhinoceroses were saved, as were the teenage elephants.

I feel Raspberry used the elephant story as a way of calling for a stronger adult male presence in the lives of teenagers. He made the point that by-in-large stable males are not present in the lives of male teenagers, especially African-American teens, and the poor behavior of teens is often looked upon as an effect of many other social ills or, as the Rochester police chief once put it, "a lack of good choices."

But all of these well-intentioned commentators have overlooked the fact that the increase of violence is now an accepted means of communication among teens and, as well as the absence of stable male role models, is a result of the national temperament turning towards colonialism and consumption. It is an extension of the trend that began at the end of the agrarian period in America and Europe when industrialization began to take the role model, along with the myths, symbols and coming-of-age rituals for adolescent transition, away from the home and plant it somewhere near the city, outside the factory, in a garbage can or in a tavern near the warehouse. Most men today will acknowledge that they leave the best part of their energy at the office, at the factory, at the construction site, on the prison yard and in the subway. Few will truthfully admit that they spend enough time, if any, with their children. The time they do spend is limited in both quality and quantity by the energy they have left from their relentless quest for economic dominance or independence.

Professor and author Joseph Campbell, in his now famous interviews and lectures, made this point as well when he talked about the role of the initiator in traditional societies. He commented that the shaman once took divinity—which always stemmed from nature—and interpreted it for the society. These interpreters were the so-called adult role models who functioned as translators for the society; the ones who taught right from wrong and managed both the short-term and long-term direction of the culture. But when journalist Bill Moyers asked Campbell who fills this role today, the man who was perhaps the most well spoken academic of his generation began to stumble a little. He had talked for many days, even years, fluently and clearly about mythology. But when asked about the role of the initiator in society today, he paused and stammered. He circled around an answer, telling Moyers that it was the job of the artist and that individuals could fill the role as well, mainly through reading and experiencing authors and other art work. But the lack of a confident answer really revealed that, as difficult a realization as this is, there really isn't anyone today who is effectively translating and interpreting the divine in our world, which is precisely why we don't recognize it or see it.

Divinity has always been associated with nature. In all traditional cultures, survival, and what has come to be known as the Mother Goddess, has been an extension of nature. The agrarian nature of ancient living was somewhat responsible for this. But if we really think about it, our world today is no less dependent on agriculture and the environment for survival. The main difference today is that we have walked backwards from the divine, have stopped acknowledging the fundamental divinity of nature and have thus lost the psychic connection to it. This is why we are able to pump somewhere in the neighborhood of a trillion pounds of carbon dioxide into the atmosphere every year from our cars and smokestacks, changing the basic composition of the atmosphere. Even as the worst hurricane season in history was pummeling the southern United States and people were swimming for their lives in a flooded

New Orleans after Hurricane Katrina, most people never made the connection between the cause of the event (global warming) and the event itself.

This lack of interaction with the divine, the Goddess, the earth, is something like a dysfunctional relationship in a family. One might say it is akin to the concept of codependence. We depend on nature for survival, in both a physical and a spiritual sense. Nature, on the other hand, relies on humanity to develop an interpretation system so that the two can have a mutually beneficial relationship. But like the dysfunctional family, we no longer communicate with nature. In fact, we no longer recognize her at all in most instances. Our cereal is bought from a store with a tin roof and cement parking lot, packaged in toxic plastic and fortified with chemicals, preservatives and artificial colors. The wheat from the field that is really the heart of the cereal is so far removed from our own experience that we can barely even recognize that it's in the box at all. This abstraction speaks to the fact that we no longer have adults, shaman, elders or anyone whose job it is to interpret nature and the divine for us or for our children.

In my opinion, Campbell was right when he said that in today's world it is the artist's job to fill this role. However, it is the artist's role by default, but most people don't recognize the artist at all. Most look at the artist as poor, disconnected from reality and pathetic. The parents meet their friends at a cocktail party and the discussion turns to their children. "Well, Ben's an aspiring *artist*," they say in sarcastic resignation. "He's waiting tables in New York City while he's waiting to be discovered!" They laugh at the pomposity of the son's pursuit.

We find ourselves in a culture that is also unwilling to accept other basic, untenable truths about our world. In my opinion, young adults cannot achieve their potential for success without the support structures of a community, internship opportunities and mythology-based coming-of-age practices. If we do not come to terms with what adolescents need to grow into responsible, caring adults, we may shut down the arts, prohibit controversial literature, do away with philosophy and wide reaching sciences and, in essence, perpetuate the horizontal mind.

①②

Wild Boys, Wild Men
and the Long Psychological Bag

One of the most enduring images on the marital landscape of human development and the inner psyche is that of the wild man. In literary treatments, ancient mythology and real life, the man who goes beyond human and into the other realm of unsatisfied desires personified has become symbolic of all those things humans have been unable to address successfully in the conscious world. In some of our stories, the wild man is combined with godliness, as in the Ganesha myth, with powerful omnipotence and deep, yet sensitive, inner longings that are not met. In other tales, such as those of various vampire and werewolf stories, we have a half-man, a goodhearted man. He is imprisoned by his dark inner monster, whose lust, or violence, cannot be successfully contained. Wild man mythology has always sought to give voice to the inner longings of the male psyche in safe mythological space.

Many men gather throughout their lives a metaphorical long *bag* filled with their repressed emotions and painful experiences that they are unable to deal with in the light of conscious examination. Carl Jung talked much about this *bag* during his career, and artists have dealt with it historically in many treatments. Child abuse is in the *bag*; a shaming or resentful father might be in there; failed marriages; the guilt of a childhood friend long ago abandoned; a lover whom we treated cruelly in college; career aspiration we never accomplished—all go in the *bag*. The *bag* is long and heavy and dark, and as we grow older, the bag becomes more burdensome, because we are always stuffing things in the bag and rarely letting things out. By the time we are in our adult years, the bag may become so heavy that we can no longer drag it about. It has become too heavy, and people are noticing that we have something dragging along behind us, emotionally, that we cannot release. People talk about us behind our backs: "That Joseph, I just don't know what's wrong with him…" Many men have a *bag* of some substance by the time they exit their teens, but often it is not recognized. It may take many years of hard inner work, therapy and even rock-bottoming experiences before the nature of the bag is revealed. Sometimes it is never revealed, and what is in the *bag* kills its owner.

Some have said that the classical mythology of the wild man, who is the metaphor for what is in the *bag*, is a mythological truth about metamorphosis and the dual nature of the personality. This interpretation essentially puts forth that the nature of the universe is change, that natural change causes inner conflict, and no matter how desperate the inner world of the person, the emotional and psychic landscape will inevitably change and evolve due to new experiences combining with past knowledge. Ovid's *Metamorphosis*, the seminal work on this theme, contains many cloistered remarks about the universe's ability to change one's psyche in order to meet challenge. We have become aware now, thanks to the work of modern psychology, that the troubling events of childhood—the abuses, the guilt, the shaming at the realization that our parents are not gods and goddesses—do not always fly out of the inner world as we enter adulthood, like candy wrappers out of a speeding car's window, but gather and simmer within, slowly accumulating over time into a tightly wound web of emotional conflict. We have discovered that when these burdens are not taken out of the metaphorical *bag* and viewed in the light, they become larger, more destructive and hungry for food. They feed off their hosts' positive energy, much like a fungus or a virus does, until they ultimately destroy their host. A majority of boys and men in the present culture are suffering because their personal and communal *bags* have become overstuffed. The media culture, the slow decline of the family, economics, politics and education have all helped to stuff the *bag* in the modern world. It is also a function of the modern world, with the changing dynamic of male and female roles, that men seem to have the most *bag*-stuffing going on now.

Many indigenous cultures understood that the bag first develops in childhood and is added to tremendously during adolescence. The disappointments of twelve and thirteen-year-olds are enormous, and in modern times these disappointments are more and more prevalent and pervasive, because there is little emotional guidance being offered in our culture. Having been a teacher who looked into the lives of his students outside of school in order to support their achievement in school, I have regularly seen more and more teenagers abandoned by their parents, both physically and emotionally. Many teens are living with grandparents, extended families, even with friends' parents. Still more lack any sort of psychic connection to their parents, who are at work, feeding their own disappointment with drugs and alcohol or simply too resigned, tired or conflicted to parent. "I don't know what to do with him anymore," they say of their troubled son at the parent-teacher conference. "I just stay out of his way now." The teenagers' disappointment and negativity is palpable. They have come to mistrust adults at a young age, because the adults who they first put their trust in have left them. Approximately 85 percent of all incarcerated men come from fatherless households. We expect to see a connection with this statistic and their criminal records. In addition, we are seeing a growing trend in the population of teens who come from father-less and motherless households across all socioeconomic classes. Not exactly orphans, they live outside the foster care and social services systems and are thus poorly documented. The Council on Contemporary Families reports that there are 1.4 million children in America with neither a father nor a mother in the household, which is a number that grows each year.

We may think that the concept of the psychological *bag* is a modern or Western concept; that tribal peoples do not have *bags* like this. But it is dangerous to over-sentimentalize tribal cultures. It may be that primal cultures have a *bag* filled with the discards of childhood that is equally as heavy as our own. However, their *bags* may contain different ingredients.

As adolescents, either we are made to feel guilty if we participate too freely, or we feel uninitiated and outcasted if we abstain. So sexuality goes in the *bag*. In some tribal cultures, there may be other influences that must be cast off into the *bag*, such as individuality that is jettisoned in favor of communal personalities. If individuality is discarded, so too is creativity, at least as practiced for personal development and exploration. Repudiating creativity can be quite destructive indeed. It may be that the fundamental nature of the *bag* and its accumulation during childhood and adolescence is multicultural and unavoidable. Likely, it isn't the size of the *bag* that differs, just the contents and the way certain cultures deal with the *bag*.

We can think of the repressions that go into the *bag* as viral cultures, something like a deadly strain of smallpox. The *bag* itself is the petri dish, or the growing medium, where the pox can flourish. The conditions in the *bag*—darkness, isolation, remoteness—are perfect for our repressed feelings to change into something ominous and powerful. Say that the teenager fills the bag while in high school, and then seals the *bag* and tries to pretend it is not there. He may drag it behind him for many years, all the while his life is eroding, his performance is suffering and his emotional growth is slowly grinding to a halt. By the time twenty years have passed, the stuff in the *bag* has taken on a life of its own; it may be so powerful now that it is ready to burst out of the *bag*. The man's marriage breaks up, he loses his job, his friends abandon him because he "just isn't in the same place" as they are any more. The things in the *bag* have become the wild man, have broken free of their containment, and are now running about, pillaging.

Some cultures honor the wild man instead of hiding his realm away in the *bag*. In one such culture, the Hindu ceremonies from the Ramayana are fierce and terrifying. The performers wear monstrous masks and make no attempt to hide their role as demons. They *want* the audience to be afraid. The Jing roles in the Beijing Opera are another example of addressing the wild man through art. These actors play the parts of the warriors, the supernatural beings and might wear high-soled leather boots that are always ready to kick someone's teeth in. But we should make a distinction here about the difference between these artistic representations and the real thing. Honoring the wild man by bringing him up into the artistic realm is healthy. It is a way of facing the dark pox that is festering both in the artist's *bag* and also in the audience's. It is safe, because no one's teeth actually get kicked in; the werewolves don't actually come and rip us apart. But allowing the wild man out of the bag unintentionally, and without proper caution and supervision, can be extremely harmful. The aggressiveness we see in the boxing ring, on the football field, in the bare knuckle fights in steel cages that are shown on television, the violence on our highways and in our streets, these are not healthy examinations of our repressions or inner psyches. It is just unchecked violence and frustration, a result of the mixture we have tossed into the bag during childhood and adolescence.

As the story goes, author Robert Louis Stevenson awoke one night startled and terrified. He complained to his wife of his dreams, which included a hairy, ape-like man who was prowling the streets with murderous intentions. He didn't know for sure if the man in his dream was himself or a stranger, but the dreams seemed quite real. Stevenson's wife encouraged him to write down descriptions of his dreams, which he did. The dreams later became the novella, *The Strange Case of Dr. Jekyll and Mr. Hyde*. Stevenson had a pretty large *bag* of his own to worry about. He was raised primarily by a nanny and likely felt the abandonment many of today's boys feel when they are not in close proximity to their parents. On top of this, he was a sickly young man, having contracted tuberculosis. As a result of his ill-health, he was at various times forced to abandon his career aspirations, travel abroad alone and seek relief in foreign lands. His loneliness gave rise to many of the characters in his stories, often pirates, stalkers or other outcasts.

Something in the story of Jekyll and Hyde tells us that the contents of the *bag* cannot just be released out into the world without being somehow metered first, perhaps by filtering back through the psyche. The creature in the story is the antithesis of Dr. Jekyll, who is formal, kind and compassionate to his patients. We know that certain people in our culture have a wild man alter ego; they are kind at times, but burst out of the *bag* as abusers when we least expect it. We sometimes call them "passive aggressive." We might also say that aside from personal wild men, our nation and other nations, have their wild men as well. Pol-Pot and the

Khmer Rouge in Cambodia were incarnations from the dark *bag* of that nation's poverty and suffering. The white regime in South Africa that caused the misery of so many of the indigenous black South Africans was another. George Bush, Dick Cheney, Donald Rumsfeld and other current and former U.S. leaders, in my opinion, who rushed into military confrontation in places like Afghanistan and Iraq are right now the fast-moving creature who kills by night and comes to the office by day dressed in a bright tie, smiling, shaking hands and patting people on the back. I believe Nixon, Kissinger and General William Westmoreland could be considered national wild man incarnations from the Vietnam era.

We might say that whole nations put their disappointments and psychic wounds into a *bag*. Perhaps given the scrutiny under which governments operate, it is no surprise how much gets put into the *bag*, how long it festers there and how much more vigorously it grows than does the personal *bag*. America's mistreatment of some of its children is one of the things, I feel, we have in our national *bag*. The failure to recognize how harmful our industrial and economic system is on our own population, to say nothing of the populations of other parts of the world, is yet another thing we've put in our bag. Television opens and feeds what's in the *bag*, because it denies our children the opportunity to learn alternatives to stuffing things into the *bag*. The alternative to *bag* stuffing is to bring our psychic challenges into the light, examine them honestly and completely on a national level, teach our children that our national posture is not perfect and attempt to reach a higher plane of national understanding and international cooperation. The *bag* dragging behind the horizontal society is so enormous, because we live in a land where television tosses us a new hero each night so that many of us never have to dive down inside our own values for personal or psychic self-examination, nor rise up in order to achieve greater heights or meet greater challenges. We need only coast along, complacent and comfortable, striding horizontally, unaware or unconcerned that our *bag* has grown far more powerful than the master who created it.

①③

Boys and Sex

Some men never advance beyond the over-sexualization of adolescence. There are many such men in America and other countries. They are never likely to be able to commit themselves to one relationship, and they often see their relationships as either conquests or dominoes forming a line that has been predetermined to tumble down sooner or later. Such men show symptoms of this in today's world, many have a fixation on objectification of women, as is demonstrable in the popularity of pornography, strip clubs and other overtly sexual practices that lack an emotional element. More and more men seem to be coming out as "sex addicts," seeking clinical confirmation of their behaviors. Actors such as Michael Douglas and Charlie Sheen have admitted to being sex addicts, and many other men have recognized this trait in their own profiles in recent years. One such man I knew was in his thirties. Successful and good-looking, Bart never married, but spent all his free time pursuing sexual conquests. Bart would state his mission for the evening with military detail: "Tonight I am going to attack X nightclub, have sex with at least one girl before midnight, and then go over Y's house for the follow-up." Bart kept a record book with over seven hundred women he had slept with, their bedroom habits and their phone numbers. He labeled the cover: "Quest for 1000."

In the horizontal society, with adults regressing toward childhood or never progressing at all toward adulthood, we are seeing much confusion among adolescent boys when it comes to relationships. Their relationships with their mothers are stressed; with fathers, the relationships are distant or nonexistent. As might be expected given these circumstances, many teenage boys are becoming less and less likely to be able to sustain meaningful, appropriate, romantic relationships as they grow older.

Modern boys experience problematic interpersonal relationships, because of the lack of both coming-of-age support and mentoring, but also because they are constantly bombarded with media and cultural messages that train them to act more like sexual conquistadores than romantic partners. In past generations there was a similar message brewing: In the 1930s, Errol Flynn was the typecast lothario of his day; Clark Gable, Elvis Presley, James Dean and many more followed. However, there are significant differences in today's world. Primarily, the negative messages are far more prevalent and the mitigating factors are far less available. Fathers and adult mentors used to combine to create a cultural message that would offset boys' urges to think of romantic interaction on a purely sexual basis. But those forces are no longer available, or at least no longer potent enough to dispel the media barrages.

One of television's most undesirable side effects is that it opens adulthood's backstage for viewing. We watch as sexual relationships are played out in every context imaginable, in thirty-minute episodes, without any study of the relationship that might be needed to form around the activity itself. Worse, the undersides of some politicians, sports heroes, clergy, anyone who might have filled the role of mentor to past generations are now flaunted in front of the cameras as their sex lives, or mistakes, are revealed and studied by the media. Opening the dark doors of adulthood's underside to young boys only builds up the distrust and misunderstanding of what adulthood really means. The model of adulthood on television is of a severely flawed adult of the Senator Larry Craig variety getting arrested for soliciting anonymous sex in an airport bathroom, former president Bill Clinton having sex with a young intern in the Oval Office, former New York Governor Eliot Spitzer inviting call girls to his hotel room or of any one of dozens of sexually charged adult-children promoting promiscuity, drug and alcohol abuse and anything but responsible adult behavior. Yet these half-adults are the ones in power, making millions of dollars, dominating the airwaves, running the government. It is no wonder what youth strive to emulate, given these choices.

As many researchers have noted, in lower socio-economic communities in particular, boys are being urged to have as many sexual conquests as possible, as young as possible, and are rewarded with acceptance if they are misogynistic and sexually aggressive in their behavior toward girls. With an ever-increasing amount of confusion among boys about how to interact with the opposite sex, shyness is being replaced by aggression. In a 2002 study by the American Association of University Women (AAUW), 83 percent of eighth through eleventh grade girls self-reported that they had been sexually harassed. We know as well that sexual violence committed by teenage boys is on the rise, and rates of other types of teen crime have grown commensurately. It all points to an increasingly confused population of boys, unsure of how to interact with girls, ignorant to partnership and nurturing and growing increasingly violent, aggressive and voluminous in the horizontal society.

While all this is going on, the adult culture is regressing toward adolescence, taking on the same aggressive, predatorial persona, and attempting to join and behave like teens. Conduct an internet search using "Teenage Boys, Teacher Relationships, News" and you will find over 1.5 million hits, many of them local newspaper stories about public school teachers ages twenty-five to thirty-five who were caught having romantic relationships with high school and middle school age kids thirteen through sixteen years old. The cases of teachers Pamela Rogers Turner and Mary Kay Letourneau are but two that captured national headlines because of their sensationalism and camera-friendly participants. But the trend is there.

Reliable studies support what we see in the news. In surveys of both teachers and students, between 10 and 14 percent have reported teacher-student sexual interaction at the high school and middle school levels. This equates to more than 32,000 incidents per year. While sex abuse by priests, especially in the Catholic sect, has grabbed many headlines recently, teacher-student sexual contact is over a hundred times more prevalent than abuse by clergy.

Adults who act like adolescents are not simple pedophiles, as media reports often portray them to be. These adults enlist in professions, such as educators, counselors and social workers, that are meant to support and mentor teenagers. Half-adults and adult-children cannot teach or protect other children. They can only interact with them as peers, and we are seeing an increasing number of schools, homes and institutions run by adult-children who are unable to distinguish their roles in the horizontal society. With no real coming-of-age process and no way for them to determine where childhood ends and adulthood begins, boys in our culture travel sideways among the children instead of upwards toward adulthood. We need only to turn on the television to see the symbolic representation of this. Every face is youthful and vibrant; if it is not, they are quick to find the nearest plastic surgeon who can provide a chemical peel, a face-lift or other interventions to make them more youthful. Presently there are not one but two reality television shows that simply follow plastic surgeons through their daily routines of helping adults look more like adolescents.

In the pre-industrial era, there was little time for adolescence, or childhood for that matter. Boys were expected to join the workforce or work about the home and farm as soon as they were able. The lessons of coming-of-age were taught on the job. By contrast, in the electronic culture, children have nothing but time, and adolescence in particular is so idealized that it is extended as long as possible, often indefinitely. In all cultural groups that can be thought of as successful, the young have accepted and perpetuated the rituals of their elders. They take the common ways and stories of their tribe and use them to teach the next generation. We are now witnessing generations of young male Americans who have rejected the successful ways of their elders and who are traveling hastily toward something new. As for the stories from the elders, some boys have decided to move as quickly as possible toward non-literacy. Boys are forming a new culture with new rituals, many with no purpose. The success of the group has given way to personal definition. As with any new culture that rejects the successful ways of its past generations, there is bound to be chaos.

The role of the artist was one of the first to disappear when our horizontal culture started traveling sideways and forwent its attempt at ascent. Like the role of the elder and shaman mentioned previously, the role of the artist was to preserve the old stories and keep the culture's successes recorded, both practically and mythologically. But in the electronic culture, art with an eye toward the past and the future has given way to media, which only has its eye on the present. Like a digital wristwatch that disregards the past and future with only an interest for this moment in time, media projects idealized views of present day. Even period movies like *Cold Mountain* and *Braveheart* show adolescent-like protagonists occupied by their own special moment, focused on their internal dysfunction, while accidentally being mixed up in cultural conflict, which they abhor. As for painters and graphic artists, graffiti-like dancing stick figures and bizarre abstract installations dominate the landscape. Not too long ago, at a top museum, one of the featured paintings was a ten-foot-high canvas simply painted all in purple—no image, story or message. A patron stood in front of it, his arms folded, a huge smile across his face. "Couldn't you just make love to that!" he said to me. "Masterful."

In television, movies and the Internet today, pornography, misogyny and relationship conflicts dominate many of the themes. Over 80 percent of the image files stored at online storage sites are pornography. Teens today clearly think sexuality is the primary aspect of adult relationships. We all know that teenage girls are dressing and acting more sexually than in past generations. Most high schools where I've worked found it necessary to send some girls home almost on a daily basis for wearing too-short skirts or showing too much cleavage. The need for sexual attention has replaced the need for romantic partnership, and teens are often unable to distinguish the difference.

We are a society that is very good at asking our children questions, but not very good at understanding the answers they give or at doing much with the information. Consequently, we beat our paddles in the water quite vigorously, but the boat never seems to move forward. The Kaiser Family Foundation and The National Campaign to Prevent Teen and Unplanned Pregnancy have done a lot of rigorous teen surveying. They have uncovered that American teens seek out relationships, have romantic relationships and are almost completely unprepared to manage the relationships they seek and find.

Seven in ten teens say that they or their friends are involved in relationships they describe as "romantic." Asked to define "healthy romantic relationships," twelve to seventeen-year-olds said they involve "love, trust, mutual respect and honesty." Teens reported that of the relationships they observed amongst their peers, nearly 70 percent were of the "healthy" type. About 85 percent of boys and girls said that they believe sex should only happen in "long-term committed relationships."

Yet while adolescents believe that they know and understand what a good romantic relationship is, few of them see a model of it, either in their homes or on the television. Moreover, even fewer teens have any meaningful communications with their parents about dating, sex and relationships.

Parents think they are doing a good job of communicating with their sons and daughters about sex. 89 percent of them report that they have had "helpful, meaningful conversations about sex, love and relation-ships with their teens." Yet 40 percent of boys report that they have never had a helpful conversation with their parents about sex, and nearly 20 percent of teen boys say they don't know anyone at all (including their parents) who serve as examples of "healthy romantic relationships." Clearly there is a disconnect between what many parents believe and what their children experience.

A few final numbers: by the time they are twenty, nearly one-third of American girls will have become pregnant says S. K. Henshaw in a report for The Alan Guttmacher Institute, and nearly four million teens each year will contract a sexually transmitted disease (STD) reports the American Social Health Association. Without question, we are seeing a generation of teenagers who believe they know what healthy relationships are, who believe they are, for the most part, practicing healthy sexual and relationship habits and who have parents who think they are communicating with their children, while at the same time we see undeniable statistics showing exactly the opposite.

At the heart of why teens misunderstand sex and relationships is the role of mentors, teachers and parents, which is now being filled by the media. The surveys show that parents think they are communicating with their children, but only a minority of kids thinks this is true. Like the colonialist invaders who dominated the indigenous cultures of the Americas by diminishing their cultural norms, the media's mega-machine has devalued parents' ability to communicate with their children. As I've indicated in earlier chapters on kids watching television, we are allowing nearly unlimited access to a technology that both retards brain development and broadcasts a single-minded message to our children, one quite different from the message parents think their children are receiving.

We know that with children, quantity overcomes quality every time. Six to ten-year-olds, for example, spend an hour and thirty-six minutes or more a day in front of some type of electronic screen that is sending them a direct message. The same children spend less than ten minutes a day in direct conversation with their parents. We have become a society both preoccupied and paralyzed by television. 99 percent of homes in America with children under the age of six have a working television, a much higher percentage than homes with indoor plumbing.

Loss and Abandonment

For boys, not having a father to talk to throughout the day, and not having a positive male role model nearby, generates feelings of loss and abandonment. Boys feel that somehow they should have older men present in their lives, and they realize emotionally and rationally that something is amiss when these older men are absent. When a boy feels abandoned, or senses that his father has rejected him, he often falls prey to outside influence. We have become a nation that buys our boys television sets and computers, places them in their bedrooms and allows our sons to spend copious amounts of time in front of these mesmerizing devices. Years go by, and the boy who is growing up becomes sullen, violent, misogynistic or horribly detached. Thousands of parents all across America are at this moment wondering, what happened to my son?

The son's sexual training comes from suggestive advertising, adult films or other explicit media where sex is a tool, nearly completely detached from the "healthy relationships" we adults think sex should be a part of. While he is in his metaphorical or physical room with popular media, adult forces he is not yet ready to understand are intercepting part of his childhood. When ten or eleven-year-old boys watch programs with graphic sexuality, premature adolescence and a mistrust of adulthood begins. This negative sexual training is inundating boys earlier and earlier, and the forcefulness behind its delivery is more powerful today than it has ever been.

We know that modern television ridicules real adulthood and mystifies real adult relationships. Boys see perpetually adolescent Homer Simpson yelling at and choking his son and the sexy Desperate Housewives sleeping with the teenage lawn boy. These are not real reflections of adulthood, but images manufactured to perpetuate an adolescent ideal to an audience that is easily manipulated. But after a certain amount of time in the media room, the line between reality and make-believe fades. The wall between humanity and artifice falls down; and the television characters' impulses of their primal instincts, destructive habits and dog-in-heat sexuality spreads throughout our children's reality.

Too many raise our children by proxy while we struggle with one-parent families, no-parent families and overworked and overstressed parents always on the go, commuting two hours, working the night shift, the weekend shift, any shift that will pay the bills. If we opt out of this cycle, we risk becoming one of the legion of American poor, living amidst drugs and violence in the ghettos and suffering substandard health care, unreliable housing and malnutrition. Modern economics have created a social and fiscal order of sorts, but complete disorder in the family.

Boys growing up in this type of family sense they have been abandoned. In some respects, they are smarter than we give them credit for, because they know on some fundamental level that society has abandoned them and that the support structures once offered by society have now disappeared. It is certainly no surprise to find their anger on the rise, their disrespect for adulthood increasing, their understanding of sexuality diminishing and their search for the simple comforts of permanent adolescence so complete.

①④

Why Today's
Schools Fail Boys

In the horizontal society, schools have become a place where many children, especially boys, learn to dislike adulthood. Modern education, put quite simply, is failing many of our boys, and also some girls, because it lacks, or knows and fails to respond to, some fundamental understandings of how boys learn, grow, develop and prosper cognitively. We can think of the school as a place where many children are destined to fail because they are, at a very young age, thrown into an environment that pits each child against others and against a system of standards that lacks elasticity. They are confronted by unbendable standards that are increasingly difficult to achieve for a majority of boys. In many states, such as New York, such rigorous standardized testing in the core subject areas begins as early as fourth grade, and without testable success in the core subjects as they grow older, students will not be allowed to graduate high school. It is a one-size-fits-all system that, I feel, does not effectively accommodate different personality types, different learning styles or the basic emotional and psychological needs of teenagers.

In a speech given to the German Informatics Society, Neil Postman states:

Another way of saying this is that a new technology tends to favor some groups of people and harms other groups. School teachers, for example, will, in the long run, probably be made obsolete by television, as blacksmiths were made obsolete by the automobile, as balladeers were made obsolete by the printing press. Technological change, in other words, always results in winners and losers.

Research has indicated that the prefrontal lobes of the human brain were the last to develop in the evolutionary spectrum and that higher-order thinking, the kind we hope to foster in our children, takes place there, not in the reptilian core of the brain's older structures. However, in many schools we force the adolescent brain to do its work in the reptilian core. In the school system, children are immediately and perpetually confronted with the stresses of standardized testing. The constant threat of "the test" throws many children, especially boys, into a state of defensiveness and fear, pushing their thought processes down away from the prefrontal lobes and into the ancient structures of the R-brain where survival instincts are dealt with. I have documented many cases of "test anxiety" in my own students. Often, many of my boy students, but some girls as well, shut down academically, sometimes refusing to even attempt answers on the tests. Other times they feign illness, intentionally miss school on test days or purposefully misbehave so that they are removed from the test room.

Darryl, one of my straight-A students, simply filled in the answer key of his state exam in a random pattern, not even bothering to attempt reading the questions. Students' anxiety drives them to seek any solution to what they perceive as a real threat. Curiously, it is not always the children one would expect to perform poorly on the tests who demonstrate the test anxiety behaviors. So many students now show test anxiety symptoms—some estimate as many as 25 percent of all students—that school counselors now build questions about test anxiety into their routine student evaluations. We in the education structure in America have developed a generation of children, especially boys, who are terrorized in school and measurably debilitated, both academically and emotionally. This is a major reason I believe our emphasis on standardized testing is too much.

We can think of the older structures of the brain as having become "settled" over vast amounts of evolutionary time. Their functions are defined, and the brain knows how and when to use those older structures, as it does so effectively during panic and anxiety situations when the brain causes the heart rate to speed up, the muscles to charge with increased blood flow and the body to find any way it can to escape. But in the prefrontal lobes the activity is different. In the new structures, evolution has not yet completed its work. The newer structures of the brain have developed, as some scientists have suggested, at a very late evolutionary date and have not yet had time to complete their development or fully define their operations. Random mutation and selectivity, as Darwin described it, has not yet had time to occur. Combine this with the knowledge that the adolescent brain is still undergoing a dynamic developmental window between about ages fifteen and twenty-one, and we can see that adolescents need educational structures that encourage the work and development of the prefrontal lobes, not the fight or flight processes in the R-brain that are encouraged under the constant stresses of standardized testing.

What adolescents need, as opposed to higher standards for mathematics, science and English, are nurturing environments filled with empathic mentors—male and female—who understand the needs of the individual over the needs of the group. In most of our schools, we treat adolescents either as an enemy or as a god whose desires require acquiescence. We do not recognize that their inherent idealism is propelling them to investigate individual interests that may relate to the core areas of study, but are not directly in line to prepare them for standardized testing. There are some schools that understand this notion. School Without Walls, for example, in the Rochester, New York, School District, once had an educational plan that required each student to propose an individual study project at the start of their high school years. Faculty mentors would then devise an individualized four-year course that would teach them the disciplines necessary to achieve success in their chosen endeavor. Each student was required to propose a culminating project that would be the core of their program. One student, Brent, wished to build an Adirondack Guide boat. His program included woodworking courses, math, engineering, map and orienteering, meteorology, chemistry and so on. Allowing students to direct their learning is one way in which the problem solving functions of the prefrontal lobes are stimulated to grow and develop.

Other schools, such as the private Waldorf Schools, have attempted to foster the vertical mind by using an arts-based education where children learn multiple disciplines through artistic gateways. Still others, aware of the public's demands for accountability, have sought to use portfolio assessments instead of standardized testing. Portfolio schools seek to deliver a broad, learner-centered curriculum that can be assessed by the student's completion of a portfolio of their work that represents their learning over a year or multi-year program. A typical student's portfolio might contain art, essays, individual reading lists, math assignments and, most importantly, a series of reflection entries where the student has the opportunity to chart their progress and identify the factors that contributed to their success or failure in each academic endeavor. Such efforts at a non-standardized testing educational system have been met with mighty resistance from the federal, state and local authorities in the horizontal society.

Recent research has shown that empathy may well be an inherited trait, not just in human beings, but in all mammals. Mice, for example, show a much higher pain sensitivity when they witness other mice with whom they have lived suffering. At the Center for Disease Control, monkeys are forbidden to see another monkey euthanized, tested or treated, because they will become highly agitated in their pens. Wild chimpanzees have been observed to show empathy when they see a fellow chimp fall from a tree. They scream out in horror or grasp and hug another nearby chimpanzee for comfort. We also know that human boys need empathic mentors in order to feel safe to learn and in order to develop their own empathy. Part of the so-called "boy crisis" in academia that has been noted by the media is the result of an absence of empathy in the horizontal society.

In recent years, boys have fallen seriously behind girls in virtually every academic benchmark in the United States. The diminishing academic achievements of boys has become so evident, and the downward trend so obvious, that many educators and government officials have begun studying the phenomenon, and the public has taken notice as well. What they are discovering is that there are several factors at work in the educational system that have fostered this trend. American schools overreacted to the data from the 1970s, '80s and '90s that showed girls' achievement lagging behind boys'. Educational systems and structures that addressed the needs of girls without acknowledging that boys' brains operate and learn differently than girls' were established. These have fostered an academic system that does not take into account the developmental, psychological or emotional differences between boys and girls. American society failed to recognize that the factors that contribute to the horizontal society are also contributing to the failure of our educational system for many boys as well as some girls.

Male students once dominated American college campuses and, consequently, corporate America. This is no longer the case. Peg Tyre's article in *Newsweek* magazine drew heavily on the work of psychologist Michael Thompson and notes that presently only 44 percent of college undergraduates are male, the first time in history that they have become the minority in undergraduate academia. In 1976, males made up 58 percent of the undergraduate student population. At many state schools, where economic and other demographic differences come more heavily into play, the current ratio of girls to boys is closer to sixty to forty. The lack of academic achievement in the male population can be traced clearly throughout the primary, middle and high school years by looking at the language progress at those developmental stages. Language development serves as an indicator for progress in other academic areas.

With many states taking a stronger stance on high-stakes testing, we are provided with much more data than was previously available. In states such as New York, children now take high-stakes standardized tests in reading and writing every one or two years. According to the United States Department of Education, girls in grades kindergarten through three are showing a much higher reading proficiency than boys, both in academic settings and at home. At ages three through five, girls are 5 percent more likely to be read to at home than are boys. As we have discussed in earlier chapters, reading to children with above level vocabulary is one of the best ways to develop the language centers in the child's brain. By the time girls reach first grade, they are 10 percent more likely than boys to be able to recognize sight words. During the same period (grades K-3) girls' reading scores improve 6 percent more than boys'. By fourth grade, girls' reading scores are 3 percent higher on reading exams than boys' and 12 percent higher on the writing section of the exams.

During this same period of time, while the reading and writing achievement of girls is increasing and outpacing that of boys, the boys are suffering from a lack of language development and overall academic progress. For example, between the ages of five and twelve, boys are 60 percent more likely than girls to repeat a grade. By fifth grade, boys are 47 percent more likely than girls to be diagnosed with emotional disturbances, learning disabilities or other speech and language impediments such as stammers, dyslexia or other deficits that require additional intervention in the school setting. Make no mistake, boys feel as though they are somewhat second-class citizens in school. Their inferiority is palpable, and they develop an identity that incorporates these feelings of inferiority. Their future academic efforts are handicapped and their self-esteem is negatively impacted because of it, in some cases for the rest of their lives.

Some researchers suggest that data shows that boys' brains develop differently than those of girls, first lagging behind in the language areas in early childhood, then falling further behind by early adolescence, but finally catching up in later adolescence. For example, by the time boys reach middle school, where they are still taking the standardized English Language Arts exams in reading and writing, girls now score on average eleven points higher than boys on the eighth-grade reading exam and twenty-one points higher on the writing exam. By senior year in high school, girls score on average sixteen points higher than boys on the reading exam and twenty-four points higher on the writing exam.

Part of the so-called "Boy Crisis," as it was termed on the cover of the January 30, 2006 *Newsweek* issue, comes from the academic world's lack of understanding of the developing brains of boys. As Dr. Bruce Perry, a Houston neurologist, put it, "We have created a biologically disrespectful model of education" that does not recognize the developmental needs of boys. The kinetic, high-energy nature of boys' brains is a characteristic difference from young girls. By age five girls typically develop sight word recognition and fine motor skills, whereas boys typically do not. In the classroom, this means that boys will struggle with skills that teachers value, such as word recognition, reading and penmanship. Moreover, boys develop more impulsivity than girls, are less likely to sit still and have less ability to control their verbal, emotional and physical responses to stimuli in the classroom. Naturally, teachers gear their lessons to the students who are more likely to comply with the teacher, a strategy that promotes learning for the girls and places the boys in a secondary position. "Boys are treated like defective girls," says Thompson, mainly because they cannot sit still, wait their turn or stay quiet to the same degree girls can.

Once the teacher in the classroom has labeled a boy as "naughty" or "noncompliant," the boy begins to see school very differently and far more negatively than he did before. A study by researchers at the University of Michigan shows that boys are becoming increasingly dissatisfied with school. Between 1980 and 2001, the percentage of school-age boys who, when surveyed, said they did not like going to school rose 71 percent. In addition to the overall trend in dissatisfaction and downward academic achievement, boys are also facing a growing array of social and emotional problems that impact their ability to learn in school. By the time boys reach high school, 22 percent of boys skip school at least once per month, most of them giving the reason that they "did not feel safe there." Figures on violence in the schools support this. Ninth grade boys, for example, are 78 percent more likely to be injured in a fight than girls. Boys ages five through fourteen are 200 percent more likely to die by suicide than girls and 36 percent more likely than girls to die by some method during these same ages.

As adults, boys who have grown up with deficiencies in reading and writing will ultimately live lives that are less open to education, less able to synthesize complex problems and essentially more horizontal. According to "Why Women Read More than Men" by Eric Weiner, adult women are far more likely than men to enjoy reading as a pastime; men reported that their most relaxing pastime was watching television. The same poll showed that college-educated women read on average twenty-five books per year, while college educated men reported reading fifteen or less.

Behind much of this might lay differences in evolutionary development in the brains of children that have yet to be fully understood or studied. Life begins far differently in utero for boys than it does for girls. Sometime during the first trimester, the male fetus begins to produce testosterone and continues to produce significant levels of this hormone throughout its time in utero. This constant testosterone bath may affect how the child learns throughout the rest of his life. For example, in a 1994 Dutch study, when males were given female hormones, their spatial skills dropped but their verbal skills increased. The presence of male and female hormones during the prenatal cycle surely imbeds many developmental traits that will impact the growing child's education. The prefrontal cortex (new brain) develops more quickly in girls than in boys. By age eleven the cortex has reached its maximum, or adult thickness, in girls, but continues to fine-tune its development for perhaps another decade. This maximum thickness occurs about eighteen months sooner than in boys. Brain scans of girls ages eleven through eighteen reveal that girls have more complex fear reactions, such as when they are shown frightening pictures, and are much more able to process information quickly and efficiently in their advanced neocortexes. Given sets of numbers and objects to match for similarity in a timed test, researchers at Vanderbilt University were able to show marked superiority in the processing capabilities of teenage girls over teenage boys, but by age eighteen, boys were performing the tests with results equal to that of the girls.

Researchers such as Nancy Forger of the University of Massachusetts at Amherst have diagrammed at least one hundred specific physical and structural differences in the male and female brains, notes Michael Gurian. One such difference (the level of the hormone dopamine) dictates that the male brain is more impulsive and less likely to learn while the boy is sitting still. The female brain develops the language areas, those being the Broca's and Wernicke's areas, much earlier than the male brain and expands these areas with advanced neural development at a younger age. Researchers also know that definitively different hormones, which negatively or positively affect language development, are unique to the male and female brain. For example, estrogen and oxytocin, which are highly present in the female brain, impact word and language cognition whereas testosterone in the male brain impacts levels of aggression and sexual energy. We also know that boys' brains operate with about 15 percent less blood flow than do girls'.

So with all of these differences in the brain and their known effects, why are we then treating the two genders as though they are the same while in the classroom? Why are we sending boys and girls to the same schools, to the same teachers and to the same courses when we know that this practice is benefiting one gender over the other? Part of the answer, I believe, lies in the education system's lack of elasticity. Put another way, many American schools are married to their old beliefs and habits and are unwilling to take a close look at what might best benefit their populations. It would be anti-thetical to the educator's mission of "progress" to revert to methods of tutoring and apprenticeship that were effective one hundred or two hundred years ago, because this would then be an admission that instead of endeavoring to serve the economic mission of the school and devote its energy to preparing students for the new economies of the technology era, schools would be regressing backwards to a previous economic belief system.

Under such curricula, boys should work in a hands-on way with older men, experience their rights of passage and assume, little by little, the responsibility of adulthood. Such regressions are intolerable in the technology-centered paradigm that controls modern education and tells children that they must grow up as quickly as possible and get on with their careers. The mere notion that boys might be better served by rising out of their desks, honoring their inborn need for activity, motion and physical movement, is antithetical to much of the power dynamic upon which schools are founded. But forcing boys to sit silently in their seats in an attempt to learn doesn't work; the numbers show this, and I observe it in the classroom every day.

As psychologist Michael Gurian has pointed out, the primary mode of instruction for male children is exactly the type of instruction that least suits their brain evolution: verbal learning groups and independent study, both of which require extended periods of physical inactivity and stillness. The former structures of education and mentoring in the patriarchal society, the tutoring, apprenticeship, field work and active learning, where boys' energy and need for activity and movement were recognized, afforded the boy the ability to meet his brain's needs while still accomplishing the learning task. Sitting still in a classroom or at a desk at home reading may not be at all effective for the developing brains of boys.

Some strikingly similar social and behavioral traits have been noted by researchers in apes and adolescent boys. Both apes and boys establish and work to maintain their role in their tribal hierarchy. This type of peer power structure comes to be one of the most powerful influences on boys in their preadolescent and adolescent years. Boys and apes in the tribal hierarchy will also choose to face off against one another, verbally or physically, and show uncharacteristic levels of aggression rather than appear weak in front of the group. Boys will refuse to admit failings or accept the need for help in dealing with their problems, almost at any cost, if such interventions may be made noticeable to the group. The extreme measures that boys go through in order to save face in front of a group may be a byproduct of the brain's constant exposure to low levels of testosterone during prenatal development. Such resistance can have profound impacts on adolescent boys in high school.

By the time they have reached ninth or tenth grade and have refused most academic interventions offered to them, boys' academic abilities are often so irreparably diminished that the only options left for them are special education classes or to drop out of school. Special education classification is such an extreme measure that it is often withheld as a last-ditch effort to get a child through school after it has become clear that he will not be able to graduate by normal means meeting the state's academic standard. Boys are twice as likely to be diagnosed with a learning disability and twice more likely to be placed in special education classes than are girls. We know that boys are 33 percent more likely than girls to drop out of high school and that only about one-half of African-American boys ever finish high school. According to Elissa Gootman's *New York Times* article, in New York State as of 2005, only 59.4 percent of all boys graduated from high school on time (four years) compared to 69.2 percent of girls. Both figures are dismally low, but the disparity between the genders is proof positive of the education system's failure to serve boys in any meaningful way. Educators are always creative in their ability to explain away students who fail, but there is no satisfactory way to explain why nearly half the boys who enter high school in New York State fail to graduate in four years.

Many believe the state of public education today is quite dismal. Pearce has called our view of education a "radical denial," and he invokes Iban Arabi's admonishment over our "enormous capacity for self denial." The call for accountability, increased funding, better teachers and new programs misses some fundamental understandings. Education in the horizontal society cannot really take place because the adults have regressed toward adolescence, and the children and adolescents want no part of adulthood. The schoolhouse has never functioned well as the space for rites of passage between childhood and adulthood. This function has always been in the realm of the village, the home or the places societies established specifically for this purpose. Rites of passage were never conducted in non-ritual spaces or in locations where adolescents congregated. Wherever groups of adolescents gather, especially where there are few capable elders to guide them, random and inappropriate initiation is bound to result, as we read about in the newspaper when a wrestling team sexually assaults a new member of the team in the locker room or when a street gang initiates a potential member by "jumping them in," or beating and kicking them when they least expect it to test their mettle. But today, society has eroded to a point where we have fundamentally abandoned any hopes of taking ownership for our young, and the school system, the most convenient of the alternatives, is left holding the bag, required under the law to take the children and make them meet certain standards, but given little support in doing so. What's more, the schools are now expected to accomplish the coming-of-age process, the sexual orientation and social initiation, and most of the other functions that the village and their mythologies and family units traditionally handled, *on top of* being held accountable for the content information of mathematics, sciences, languages, etc. Beyond this, the school must accomplish its initiation and academic tasks in an environment that does not recognize the psychological, physical or emotional differences between boys and girls, nor has any appreciable understanding of the way the adolescent brain develops or the things the brain needs to move forward, upward and beyond failure and stasis.

Most everyone inside the education system knows that the task is impossible. Teachers are asked to work sixty or more hours a week, handle larger and larger classes, plan more and more lessons and meet ever increasing standards of accountability, all while being some of the lowest paid and least respected professionals with their level of education in the nation. In New York and many other states, for example, teachers are required to obtain a master's degree in order to become permanently certified to teach, yet the average salary of a credentialed teacher in America, according to the American Federation of Teachers, is $46,597.00, far less than that of similarly educated professionals in other fields. As of a 2003-04 report, teachers gained only eighteen cents in compensation for every new dollar of earnings compared to workers in the private sector. But it is not only the lack of economic incentives that prevent successful instruction from happening in our schools. There are many causes and concerns: poverty, the shattered family, high-stakes testing and many others that are well documented and discussed in many, many books. But as a teacher, I can attest—and I think many in the field would agree—kids are not learning in the same ways, or through the same methods, as previous generations. Their behaviors are different; their needs are different; their brains are different. No matter how dedicated teachers are to using "best practices" in the classrooms, there is little that can be done when 20, 30 or even 60 percent of the students in the school are not *capable* of learning at the expected levels. Children today have developed brains that are malnourished, and much like the body that does not build strong bones or powerful connective tissues when it is fed only donuts and soda pop while growing up, so, too, the brain does not do well on a diet of television, video games and broken families.

The young in any culture need good brain food: meaningful stories, a connection to the living history of their people, knowledgeable elders and a mythology created especially for their particular needs. The modern age provides none of these, least of all in the school systems. It is no wonder that many young boys and girls today hate school and find its only redemptive quality the opportunity to join a peer group that bands together around hatred of the adult world and its authority.

In the past, the rebellious feelings of the young were repressed by the paternal culture that stressed respect for one's elders and a need for conformity. Later, some of the rebelliousness was honored, as James Dean and Elvis demonstrated in the 1950s and the Woodstock generation lovingly embraced in the 1960s. But there was a transition of sorts from the 1960s until the 1990s, when new ideas about education were attempted, the notion of a child-centered curriculum was approached and multiple learning styles were recognized. But this individualization of academics and the culture's horizontal stretching led by popular media have resulted in too much honor being placed upon the rebellious spirit of adolescence. In 2000 and beyond, no longer are children's complaints about school tolerated as an annoyance or ignored as was done in the paternal culture, but, in many schools, unfounded complaints are now honored and discussed at school board meetings. "They (the students) don't like to read Shakespeare anymore," said one board member at a recent meeting. "We really ought to think about taking it out of the curriculum. *Way* too boring."

Today, children who complain to their parents or their principal that "the teacher is too hard on us" are often coddled and mollified, and the teacher is often reprimanded. When a teacher limits socialization time and instead demands that students practice writing or silent reading, the response from the students and the school administration, in turn, is outrage directed at the teacher. Instead of the principal telling the student to get work done instead of socializing, the principal reprimands the teacher for not honoring the social needs of the student and for not understanding the demands on the child's time. "How dare you make them read!" becomes the mantra. "They hate reading. Play a learning game or something. They're not engaged enough." Teachers hear these commands all the time. Because the power structures in the school community are comprised of adults regressing toward adolescence, they see the child's complaints with validity. "I wouldn't want to do that either," they think. Children and permanent adolescents have taken authority over the schools by popular demand.

At some point in the adolescent cycle, many children lose their feelings of guilt. This is a new characteristic of the modern generations. There was once a time when children could still be rationalized with on an emotional level. For example, a child hits or kicks another child in the classroom and is sent to the principal. In past eras, the principal would appeal to the child's deep-seated sense of right and wrong and their instinct of guilt and honor. "You shouldn't have kicked Jimmy. How would you feel if someone kicked you in the shin?" The child would feel honest empathy and consolation for the victim, and their guilt instinct would demand that they act appropriately by apologizing and expressing remorse and a willingness to change their behavior. But today's children no longer maintain a firm ministry of guilt inside of them. They are committing acts far worse than kicking, spitting and name calling, and when they are called in front of the guilt officer and their remorse is appealed to, some chuckle at the principal and say, "Fuck you." As a teacher, I've experienced this many times. While monitoring the hallway outside my classroom, I may notice a student kicking, spitting on or bullying another. "Stop it, right now," I'll tell the child authoritatively. "Fuck you," the kids say back with genuine contempt. I'll call the child's home and speak with the parent. They sometimes say, "Yeah. What else is new? He says the same thing to me. There's nothing we can do." Or worse, there's no answer at all on the other end of the line.

In many instances during my time in American high schools and middle schools, the lack of a ministry of guilt has been displayed in a series of alarming incidences. In one, during the first few weeks of the school year, a small group of twelve- and thirteen-year-olds were caught smoking marijuana in the dugout on the baseball field behind the school. The teens were investigated and interviewed and gave school officials and police the names of their drug suppliers, who were also students at the school. A few days later, as two of the young girls who had been involved in the drug incident were walking home, a fifteen-year-old boy approached them while still on school property, stuck a pistol in the girls' faces and told them that if they told the police anything more, he would kill them without a second thought. Judging by the cold look in his eyes and obvious readiness, the boy was quite prepared to shoot both of the young girls. The incident was reported and the boy was suspended from school for a few weeks. In another incident, the assistant wrestling coach was making his athletes run laps around the gymnasium at practice. One boy, a sixteen-year-old, stopped and panted, not wanting to go on. "Come on, Ronnie," the coach commanded. "Get back in line and finish your laps." The sixteen-year-old walked up to the coach and screamed, "Screw you fat ass!" The wrestler was sent home from practice, but was reinstated to the team the next day after a half-hearted apology was passed along via another teammate.

Such incidences are but a few in a long and growing trend of young people who no longer grow up with the ministry of guilt inside of them. With an established understanding of consumerism, numerous adolescents are only looking for what they can take—be it the silence of other students, a spot on the wrestling team, good grades without hard work or whatever else might be there for the taking without fear of persecution. Today, the guilt index inside many children is largely missing.

①⑤

Teaching Boys in
the Electronic Culture

Early childhood education, primary school, grade school and high school are largely feminine environments set up to teach to the way girls learn. They are dominated by female teachers and create instruction that ignores the dynamic, high energy and active personality of most boys. This ignorance of male brain chemistry puts boys at a disadvantage early on. The girl-centered approach came about for a number of reasons and was reinforced with an ever-increasing emphasis on standardized testing that requires large amounts of rote learning and memorization in the classroom. Sitting still and listening to an instructor speak for long periods of time is contrary to the way boys learn.

I believe it is patently unfair to pit boys against girls for equality in the classroom. In such an approach there will be winners and losers, and we do not want one gender to lose in the quest for education. We want all winners. Some educators have begun to take a closer look at the value of same-gender education and why segregating boys and girls in school might have value. Boys spend over a thousand hours a year in school, and the relationships they form with teachers and classmates are as valuable as any curriculum content they may learn. So it doesn't seem quite right to promote same-sex education or same-sex instructors exclusively. But same-sex education may have some merits if used wisely. In primary and elementary school, approximately through grade six, the active brain development of boys creates biological conditions that encourage active learning. At this age, they are driven to get out of their seats and move around, to shout, to touch things with their hands and to socialize with their peers, who, at this age, are largely same gender. In many primary school dual-gender environments, a great deal of focus is placed on learning to sit still, to quietly listen, to organize and to focus. These are exactly the skills that the growing male brain and body are screaming out against.

I have worked in schools that experimented with same gender education in grades seven through twelve. The boys' classes self-reported that they had fewer distractions, and, with male teachers, they could freely discuss personal issues such as sexuality, hygiene and relationships that they would have never approached in dual-gender classrooms. They were also able to enjoy more active learning, more hands-on math and science instruction and greater interaction with their classmates than in the dual-gender classrooms. But at the same time, the boys reported that they were deeply disappointed in the same-gender environment for just the reason that they signed up for it in the first place: a lack of girls. Somehow they understood that they were learning better but missed having girls around. Clearly, the hormone factor is too powerful in the upper grades to allow same-gender classrooms and schools to achieve the successes they enjoy in the lower grades.

Aside from the biological development that encourages boys to be active learners, there is growing evidence that dual-gender learning environments, especially in grades kindergarten through three, actually retard the emotional development of boys. Multiple studies have shown that early success in school is a predictor of long-term academic success for both boys and girls. This goes along with our understanding of brain development at the younger ages. But on an emotional level, boys in the presence of female classmates in environments dominated by female teachers are encouraged to keep their emotions bottled up, on hold or altogether hidden. When upset, they are told not to yell and scream, to control themselves and not to cry out loud. But when a five, six or seven-year-old boy is told that his emotions—emotions he doesn't understand to begin with—are invalid or problematic, it creates a great shame in him. This shame deepens, because the emotions don't go away; they are developing normally and will come to the surface in most boys on a regular basis at this age. However, it is his understanding of these emotions that is being crippled. He soon comes to feel as though his normal emotions are inappropriate and believe that there is something fundamentally wrong with him. The hidden hurt and disgrace many boys feel by the time they reach third grade is immense, especially if their parents reinforce the school's message that their fear, sadness, confusion or anger should be well-controlled and hidden from view. We talked earlier about the long bag that many men carry behind them. Early childhood is a time when a lot of things get shoved in the bag, especially during the school day.

This significant lack of emotional development along with emotional misunderstanding and shame sets boys up to fail in school. By third grade many boys have already given up on school, viewing it as a place where they feel as though they can do no right, and they have written off their chances of success in a school environment. This early resignation can be a powerful force and is a consistent predictor of long-term academic failure, depression and even suicide.

Boys need to feel physically and emotionally competent in order to invest in their education. The best way to help boys succeed in school is to help them feel that they can be successful at what they are doing. This includes understanding their lack of impulse control, lack of maturity relative to girls and their need to be active. Schools, teachers and parents who create encouraging environments that allow for these gender differences can support the emotional development of boys. Soon, we find, if boys' emotional selves are supported, their academic achievement often follows.

Eliminating the Inferiority Complex

The majority of boys reach developmental milestones much later than girls. My daughter was speaking in complete sentences at twelve months. My son is two and can barely put two words together. "Bapple juice!" he pleads. Not recognizing these developmental differences between boys and girls creates an inferiority complex in many boys that is tenacious and strikingly difficult to overcome.

A student of mine named Ricky was experiencing great difficulty in ninth grade. Ricky was a good-looking kid, had many friends in school, participated on the wrestling team and didn't get into any more trouble than the average boy his age. But his grades were deplorable. By the end of the first quarter, he was failing English, Global History, Math and even Physical Education. His mother and stepfather pleaded with me and his other teachers to help them address their son's academic problems. They were distraught because although he had never been a great academic success, Ricky had always gotten by.

Before meeting with his parents, his teachers met, looked through his file and discussed commonalities in Ricky's classes. We all noted that he seemed reluctant to learn, unable to concentrate and he came up with a myriad of excuses why he didn't get his work done or didn't come to class. He regularly needed to go to the nurse during math class because of mysterious stomach aches, and his dog always ran off with his essays.

But I thought that I might have an insight into Ricky's problems that the others in the group didn't have, and I spoke up to say that I thought that night's get-together was a mistake. Schools and parents often attempt to use scare tactics with teenagers. They use outside motivators, threats really, to encourage students to work harder, often mistakenly assuming that the child's lack of success is contributable to effort alone. In Ricky's case, his teachers were planning to convey the consequences of failing ninth grade, and we were going to threaten to remove him from the wrestling team if he didn't step up the pace; his parents had other consequences at home that they were preparing to deliver. But I didn't think Ricky's problem was lack of effort alone. I suspected that he was suffering from a deep inferiority complex, caused mainly by a lack of language arts skills that made him feel as though he couldn't be successful in school.

I knew Ricky had poor language development, and his record of testing supported this. His verbal scores were consistently lower than his quantitative skills throughout his academic record. But in early grades, school administrators are somewhat handcuffed as to how to help students such as Ricky. He wasn't quite weak enough to qualify for special education services, and holding boys back in the lower grades can be virtually impossible. I had spoken with Ricky several times privately throughout the period that I had been his English teacher, and I knew from his comments that, as he put it, "I just don't get it, when I read some of these things."

In high school level language arts courses, one of the main skills that teachers encourage is reading comprehension. Students are taught to read complex, multi-level nonfiction and literature and to separate the information into content areas using charts, organizers and other tools; then students are asked to interpret the meaning of the information and respond to it. This is the typical format of state tests in the language arts area. But I could tell Ricky couldn't make heads or tales of complex written information, and I knew that the tasks were reinforcing his already damaged self-image and self-worth. He had reached a point where the work had become intolerably hard, the support minimal, and Ricky, in a manner of speaking, threw in the towel.

We often read about male sports stars in the newspaper who excel in college athletics, reach the pros and then reveal that they never learned to read. In part, this is because today's schools are arranged to make kids successful at any cost. Nothing reflects more negatively on a school district than low graduation rates, and I have seen school administrators graduate students who have both never attended certain required courses and who were caught red-handed cheating on final senior exams. Ricky was in this category as well. He hadn't kept up with his classmates in the lower grades, had developed low self-esteem because of it, but had been moved up through the grades without anyone having ever addressed the underlying problems.

Educators Arthur Costa and Bena Kallick have developed a very insightful learning process that addresses the learning needs of boys such as Ricky. Their program is called "Habits of Mind." The Habits of Mind program, instead of focusing on content area curriculum, teaches students critical thinking and problem solving skills that are applicable to many disciplines. Strategic reasoning, perseverance, inquiry, data gathering and resolution evaluation are some of the key skills taught to students through their program.

Teaching boys to develop critical reasoning skills and to confront problems with a reliable process of evaluation is far different than asking them to learn a specific skill. Learning to investigate and solve problems is a multidimensional skill that can be applied to nearly every conflict in life, whereas the narrow skills defined in standardized testing do not allow for creative solutions. In this context, it is easy to see how inquiry-based learning like the Habits of Mind program complement the way boys' brains work instead of working against their natural biological condition.

In the pragmatist-dominated educational model in America, we have conservatively narrowed learning to a short list of answers. There is but one way to solve a math problem we tell students; "Learn it the right way or you won't pass the test!" we tell them. The same is true for most subjects in middle and high school. Standardized tests don't allow graders to evaluate a student's problem solving skills or their tenacity at inquiry. We are only able to grade the answer as right or wrong. The potential for achievement when focusing on learning habits instead of narrow answers is incredible.

Habits of Mind focuses on educational values, such as persistence, impulse management, active listening, metacognition, questioning, applying past knowledge and gathering data through multiple senses. Such habits include a mixture of art and science, finite skill and creative expression. Such inquiry-based learning spurs more investment on the part of male students, because they are employed in actively seeking solutions, instead of being told the answers are already defined.

In the lower grades, private schools such as the Waldorf Schools focus on supporting creative learning, where children are encouraged to explore through the arts and other topics of interest to them. Mythology, folk tales, song and performance, instead of being off-limits or a short distraction, are fundamentally respected as part of the inquiry-based learning that children, especially boys, can relate to. Learning through multiple channels is amazingly motivating to a pre-adolescent boy. By consciously trying to feed the imagination, the Waldorf program seeks to blend the scientific mind with the artistic mind. The result is children who are far more motivated to be successful in their education than public school students.

Also in Waldorf's model, teachers are viewed as long-term mentors to their students. Ideally, they teach multiple grades and follow their students for many years, becoming involved in their lives on a personal level, instead of simply an hour per day for a certain grade year. This type of commitment encourages an equal response from the students; they see long-term commitment from their teachers and they tend to return it. Long-term commitment, or commitment of any kind, is something that modern adolescents realize all too well is missing from modern adult-child relationships.

We might say that the symbolic end to the influence of primary cultures in America came in 1911, near California's Mount Lassen, where the so-called "last wild man" was discovered wandering in the bush. The whites called him Ishi, and he was placed in a California museum where tourists could come to view this last living remnant of North America's primal cultures. Ishi was either a Yahi Indian or of mixed native North American heritage and was reluctant to communicate much about his background. He was said to be a friendly, affable and an all-around happy man, even though he was the last of his people and was put on display in an unnatural environment. Some time after Ishi joined modern culture, his handlers took him around San Francisco to see the marvels of the modern age. He was brought to restaurants, to the opera and to see the cable cars on the streets. Finally, he was taken to Golden Gate Park to witness a great marvel of the white man: Harry Howler taking off in his airplane.

We can barely imagine how startling the days leading up to the airplane encounter must have been for a man who had spent his entire life in the bush as a member of a primary culture. The handlers were expecting Ishi to drop from amazement at the sight of the flying machine. Somehow, they seemed to have wanted to convey how powerful and important modern culture was. But when the airplane took off and flew over their heads, Ishi looked up at "the white man in the sky" and burst into uncontrollable laughter. He simply couldn't believe, it seemed, the folly of these people. We can imagine that laughter to be of the sort that comes from witnessing absurdity and sadness combined. With that incident, perhaps, the last of the original mythologies of North America flew off into the clouds forever. We can imagine Ishi looking up at the plane's smoke trail and seeing the pollution, chaos and infirmity of modern culture all condensed into a streak of smog across the morning sky.

Many things are missing for boys in modern education systems, and much has gone wrong with our theory and practice of teaching boys. But as Joseph Campbell pointed out many years ago, the stages of development and the need for boys to transfer from dependency to independence is the same today as it was in ancient times. But instead of acknowledging that in many ways maturation remains the same, we have chosen to think that because technology and modernity have progressed, we must throw out all of the old ways and replace them with what we believe are practices more suited to modern, pragmatist, industrial ideals. "How could the ways of inferior peoples a thousand years ago be applicable today?" we have asked ourselves in the John Dewey era. The answer we came up with was clear: They couldn't be.

But mythology, for one thing, can still serve the same role as it did in pre-industrial cultures. Unfortunately, the pace of modernity has become so rapid that mythology cannot keep up and, consequently, has been left behind. For thousands of years myths and stories served to define for humans our relationship with nature, our understanding of science, our ethical order and our role as human beings in relation to each other and our world. We can easily see that if we look at the success of these understandings in modern culture, we have commensurately failed to maintain any meaningful process for understanding these problems through our educational system.

In primary cultures, we notice that their belief system contains, at a minimum, some sacredness—things that are godly, or holy, and cannot be manipulated by man. Looking deeper, many of the things that primary cultures viewed as supernatural were, or are, really only elements of the natural order: our treatment of the planet, our support of our children, our dedication to our people and community. A strong argument has been made by Joseph Campbell and others who say that by intentionally dissolving our belief in mythology, symbol and ritual, we have also dissolved our commitment to the sacredness of children, family and environment. The "new mythology" of popular culture, spawned from television, movies, political rhetoric and clergy, are known to be inauthentic on many levels and will never hold the power that the sacred mythology of original cultures did.

Between mythology and humanity lies an interpreter. Tribal leaders, shaman and cultural elders interpreted the sacred mythology that guided primary cultures. Today, we have an inferior and far more confusing mythology—a pop-culture mythology that is increasingly pervasive and dangerous—and at the same time, we have few meaningful artists, elders or mentors who are able to successfully interpret it for our youth.

①⑥

Curricula for
Boys' Learning

In the failing schools, mythology and storytelling must be sneaked in surreptitiously, mainly because there is a deep and unforgiving pressure to achieve standards set by state and federal governments at any cost. The No Child Left Behind legislation of 2001 has been a disaster for many underperforming schools, especially those in high-poverty areas. The act essentially punishes poor schools that do not meet the performance standards of schools in higher-net-worth neighborhoods. The act may even take away funding from schools that do not raise their achievement. Often, these schools are left to face a crisis built upon a crisis: their districts are poor and have little in the way of a tax base to support the economic well-being of the school. Poor areas have more problems that affect school performance, such as drug abuse, lack of family support, etc. Such schools are then punished by having their already diminished resources taken away if they do not meet educational standards that are impossible for them to meet in the first place.

In schools such as these—and there are many—the administration is so focused on the dire need to improve test scores that their entire curriculum is turned over to a test preparation course. If teachers want to give the children some good brain nutrition, meaningful stories and activities that foster aesthetic thinking, they must do it in sly and covert ways. One way to do this is to take meaningful, multicultural myths and stories and use them to teach test taking skills such as reading comprehension. An example of such a story is Vashanti Rahaman's "The Man Who Could See Elephants." It's a quick and easy read for most eighth graders, yet it deals with some of the fundamental knowledge young adults need. Rahaman was born in Trinidad, in the West Indies.

She begins: "Deep in the mountains, near an out-of-the way village, there was an abandoned stone quarry. And near the quarry lived an old man who could carve the most extraordinary elephants out of stone." People came from all around the world to see them.

First Rahaman establishes a cultural context with the importance of the older artist, then a boy who is a young sculptor comes to the old man and asks him to show the boy how to carve elephants, and the old man consents.

The boy practices in a sort of internship for months, and then his teacher tells him that his internship is complete. Protesting that he has not yet learned to carve elephants, the boy convinces the old man to let him continue in his internship. The two pass the hours, the boy staring at the old man, the old man staring at the blocks of stone, looking for elephants. The boy declares he does not see elephants in the blocks of stone, and the old man explains "They are in the stone. You see, I do not carve elephants. I only carve stone."

Lastly, the young man surpasses his teacher in a way:

> The young man smiled. "I do not see an elephant," he said. "In that block of stone I see a tiger."
>
> And picking up his tools, the young sculptor went to work to set the tiger free.

I believe the story's themes are important in any process for educating young adults:

The young should aspire to learn from the society's elders.

Seeing the world figuratively and aesthetically with multiple levels of meaning should be our preferred method.

Through hard work and effort, the student should be able to eventually surpass the teacher.

We mentioned earlier how difficult it can be to reach up vertically when nearly everything in our culture honors and extends the horizontal plane of thinking, a plane of mediocrity and complacency. Reaching up psychically can be doubly difficult for children who do not yet have the impulse control in their thought process necessary to evaluate decisions about what stories to dive into. Children, and especially boys, thus need stories that open doors to their imaginations and invite them in; simple stories that are profound in their meaning.

Stories carry both the literal teachings that connect to the scientific mind and the figurative and metaphorical inferences that connect to and develop the artistic mind. Rahaman's story gives us an example of both. There are lessons contained about the need for children to respect and trust their elders as well as the inferences of the art being buried in the stone, awaiting the artist's touch, instead of being already accomplished and waiting for any child to log onto the internet and print it out. The story shows the potential for artistic achievement in any young adult's life. Figurative and metaphorical learning is one of the highest practices in education, because it demands the brain fill in unknown areas of knowledge, both with known and unknown information. These "knowledge gaps" are the places that the brain strives to fill. The evolution of the neocortex, as young as it might be, has implanted a longing to fill these gaps, and all meaningful development, both in the world of math and science as well as in the inner, cognitive realms, has been a result of this ingrained urge for the brain to fill in the unknowns. It is a very different type of learning than memorizing something already understood.

Traditional stories, including the Greek, Celtic, Arthurian, Native American, Chinese and African myths, are still present in the middle school and high school curriculums in America; however, they are dying out quickly in favor of more horizontal types of language learning.

Ministries in Children

This is probably a good time to talk about the ministries that establish themselves within adolescents. The old Soviet Union, with its communist doctrines that controlled all facets of everyday life, had "ministries" for just about everything. There was the Ministry of Tourism, which regulated travel; the Ministry of Natural Resources, which controlled the coal and oil industries; and of course there was the Ministry of Defense, which built and maintained nuclear weapons, invaded Afghanistan and helped perpetuate the Cold War. Similar ministries establish themselves within the adolescent and function much like those in the old Soviet Union once did, as a way of controlling its citizens' behavior through a doctrinal belief system. We talked earlier about the ministry of guilt, which has diminished substantially in the twenty and twenty-first centuries. Two others, the ministry of ambition and the ministry of resignation, become supremely important around age thirteen in helping the adolescent to deal with his fast-changing brain functions and his increasingly complicated environment.

The ministries of resignation and ambition compete for the adolescent's allegiance. At times, children are timid and find it easier to lie in bed late into the day with the blankets up over their heads rather than venture out into the world. But in other cases, the ministry of ambition controls the day. Teenagers often see themselves as being at the edge of a grand journey leading to greatness, godliness, genius and fame. Their worlds are replete with possibility, and no matter the challenge, there seems to be an inner voice that promises fantastic things: "You are an artist and are going to be recognized by the world as history's greatest painter" or other such assurances. As I've mentioned, teens, especially boys, will often feel emotionally linked with famous film stars, musicians, writers or pop culture icons. They may write them personal letters with much revealing information and become despondent when the star doesn't respond in kind. Teens in the grasp of the ministry of ambition find it easy to see themselves as undiscovered stars or mighty intellectuals yet to be recognized by the world.

Today it seems as though the ministry of resignation is firmly gaining control over boys' as well as girls' services and psyches, especially in the realm of education. Kids used to see education as a grand opportunity to be whatever it was they wanted. But since today the social institutions have lost much of their attractiveness, especially for many boys, adolescents, especially those on the margins of academic competence, no longer see the value in educational pursuits. I see kids every year—many of them, in fact—who simply refuse to do any schoolwork whatsoever. The former consequences of such defeatist behaviors are no longer up for consideration. I might sit a child down and tell them, "If you keep this up, you are going to fail and you will be held back next year and have to take the courses over."

"So what?" they reply. "Who cares?"

Their parents are called and told of the child's resignation and defiance. So often I hear the parent say something along the same lines. "I know, I know. I've tried. What can I do? They won't listen to me either." The ministry of resignation has become the dominant administrator in the lives of many adolescents today.

In the old, pre-industrial society, the ministries of aspiration and resignation were both kept in check by societal boundaries. Children did aspire to be successful, but much of it was because of a feeling of commitment and wanting to please the parent. The ministry of aspiration drove them to want to be like the parent. Male children wanted no more than to be in the fields with their fathers, out hunting together, fixing barns and digging wells. Girls were respectful of their fathers, probably to a fault, and idolized their mothers for their courage and wisdom. Such aspirations have all but disappeared today. Even on university campuses, many of the academic pursuits are either solely focused on economic ends or have lost any connection to the psychic realm altogether.

Cloning, crime scene investigation and chemical engineering are a few good examples of newer scientific pursuits that every aesthetic instinct screams out against in horror, yet they have worked their way into the ministry of aspiration in young people.

The Judgment of Paris

The Greeks developed a mythology to address the development of the ministries of aspiration and resignation in their young. In *The Judgment of Paris*, we find a "famous and intriguing story which is claimed to be the cause of the great Trojan War," says Steve Eddy of www.livingmyths.com, and a story that helps explain adolescent self-determination. The adolescent Paris runs up against his first sexual conflict in a meeting with three powerful adult goddesses: Hera, Athene and Aphrodite. The story begins at a wedding, where the goddess of chaos and conflict, Eris, in a tantrum throws a golden apple in the middle of the table where the three beautiful goddesses sit. The apple is inscribed "For the Fairest." Not wanting to be forced to choose one goddess over another, Zeus enlists young Paris to make the selection.

On the appointed day, Paris is first visited by the radiant Hera, who promises him bountiful gifts of wealth and power if he gives the apple to her. Paris' ambition is mighty, and the offer is considerable, but he declines, hoping for a better offer from the remaining goddesses.

Next to visit young Paris is Athene, who offers unlimited glory, wisdom and victory in battle. Again, the offer is enticing, and power is a deep draw for all young men, but Paris still denies her the apple because he wants to hear the final offer from Aphrodite.

Finally, his moment comes and Aphrodite pays him a visit. She is beautiful, with long flowing hair and a perfect figure. She quickly disrobes in front of Paris, exposing her breasts. She offers Paris all of the most beautiful women in the kingdom who will teach him love-making, and without even taking a moment to consider, Paris gives her the apple. As promised, Aphrodite delivers the most beautiful woman in all of the kingdom, Helen.

But now Paris has more problems than he imagined. Both Hera and Athene, powerful goddesses in their own right, are furious with him for his snub. But also, Helen is married to the powerful Menalaus, and so begins the ten-years' war between the Trojans and the Greeks, a war in which Paris himself lost his life.

Paris, in the Greek story, is the embodiment of teenage beauty and overactive hormones. But in the original telling of this story, I believe, Paris' painful consideration of all of the aspirations potentially afforded by the three goddesses would have been emphasized. Athene's promise of victory, glory and wisdom might have easily been overlooked by Paris because his ministry of aspiration had already assumed that he had privilege to all three of these, and already possessed some of the power, glory and wisdom promised by the goddesses. Aspirations in adolescents are often misinformed because the ego, having not yet developed sufficient countermeasures, assumes all is not just possible, but have already been afforded without much hard work. This assumption can set children up for tremendous disappointment in their twenties and thirties.

We might almost be better off calling the ministry of aspiration the *ministry of misinformation*, because it will send the wrong signals to adolescents about their potential in the new world. Kids feel that by completing high school or college, they are automatically entitled to all of the keys to the closet filled with gold: family, career, comfort, glory and esteem. But in the post-industrial world in which we live, with its stern economic and social realities, these rewards are becoming scarcer and scarcer, regardless of the amount of effort put into earning them. Athene's offerings, for all their merit, were probably the easiest for Paris to dismiss.

Hera's temptations, that of power and wealth, were likely much more enticing, especially because of who offered it. Hera, as we recall, was Zeus' wife. Sometimes brutal and vengeful, Hera was the most powerful deity Paris would have known. The ministry of resignation often looks at powerful adults in the modern world with either a position of indifference or awe. The teacher in the high school may be looked upon with scorn; the managing partner at the law firm may be looked upon as the power-giver. The new associate might even open doors for him, or wait until he has left before he enters the men's room. Paris' story warns about both of these approaches, because they come from the perspective of a society that does not provide powerful, older men and women who are at the same time benevolent and willing to mentor the culture's young. Paris' lack of control of his ministry of aspiration—in this case his sexual aspiration—caused the Trojan War as well as his own death. Children and young adults in our culture who have no mentors fare badly as well.

It is no surprise that Aphrodite wins the contest by flashing her breast and promising Paris a lover. We all know the power of desire in teenage boys. But it is meaningful that the story, like many of the Greek myths, provides severe consequences for acting on those desires without proper moderation. Children, especially in America, today become sexually aware, and sexually active, at the youngest ages in history. The regression of development in our society has affected not just the brains of young men and women, but also their bodies. We know that the average age of menses, for example, has steadily declined in the modern era. Some medical doctors have even coined a term (precocious puberty) to describe the growth of breasts in five and six year old girls. Howard Kelly of Johns Hopkins University, in his 1928 text called *Gynecology*, gauged the average onset of puberty in girls to be 13.9 years. Researchers have noted a decreasing trend in menses onset of about four months per decade. The average age of onset in America is now about age 12.6. Of course, environmental and nutritional factors are identified as part of the reason for this trend, but in a world where everyone is regressing, adult sexuality is now commonplace in children.

Some have hypothesized that we are bringing about premature sexuality in part due to nutritional additives that have entered the food chain since World War II. Just after the war, growth hormones, which were originally developed to aid food production as part of the war effort, started to be added to livestock feed to increase egg production in chickens and add size to beef cattle, hogs and lamb. The results were wildly successful, and in a few short years producing milk, eggs and meat became almost twice as easy, and twice as profitable, than before the hormones came into widespread use. The hormones, however, essentially increased the rate of development and puberty in children who consumed them through the food chain. At about the same time, Americans began a fast transition away from using human breast milk to feed their babies and began to rely on mass-produced formula for infant nutrition. Such formulas got their proteins from the milk, egg and meat products produced by the hormonally drenched agriculture and farming industries. The trend in early menses began about the same time and it is likely no coincidence.

In the West, the adult world continues to thrust adult sexuality onto its children at younger and younger ages, while at the same time our children are achieving adult milestones much later in life. Sociologists often define adult milestones as things such as full time employment, economic independence and domestic partnerships. But in the United States these outward signs of adulthood are being put off later and later in the lives of young people while at the same time the average age of menses in girls and first sexual contact in boys is dropping. In the United States, 23 percent of all fourteen-year-olds and 30 percent of all fifteen-year-olds have already had first intercourse, and studies show that sexual activity among increasingly younger teens is on the rise across all demographics, Ilana Nossel of Advocates for Youth says. The normalization of sexuality in our teens and pre-teens is reflected on television, where reality shows often group young men and women into fancy houses (*The Real World*), isolate them on islands (*Survivor*) or otherwise shove them together as we watch with cameras in every room while they interact and pursue opportunities to copulate. With an ever-present media encouraging promiscuity, and with no discussion of the responsibility and consequences of sexuality, the message teens receive is, "Do it and don't worry about it." It is another example of the adult world abandoning its duty to educate the adolescent world, and the adolescent world choosing the adult behaviors that suit them without accepting the adult responsibilities that come with them.

Teenagers' attitudes about sexuality and the resulting teen pregnancy problems are often misrepresented in the media and government reports. It is true that teen pregnancy in the United States has undergone a steep decline in recent years. However, the Alan Guttmacher Institute states that there are still about one million teenage girls in the U.S. who become pregnant each year (that's 10 percent of all girls between ages fifteen and nineteen). Of teenage girls, only about 65 percent use contraception during first intercourse, and more than three million teenagers will this year acquire some type of sexually transmitted disease. These figures show that in the United States there is a serious and growing disconnect between the action and the consequence—as will result whenever the mind meets with difficulty in projecting its decisions into future outcomes. Without the ability to blend metaphorical consequence in the mind, teenagers cannot manage powerful adolescent desires. America has a teenage pregnancy rate twice as high as England or Canada, and nine times as high as in Japan.

As in the case of violence, teenagers learn about sexuality not from adult mentors, but mainly from popular culture and peer culture. On television, sex is often portrayed as consequence-free and liberating. Corporations use teen sexuality as a marketing tool; they package it and sell it back to teenagers in the form of magazines, movies, clothing, music, deodorant and any number of other products that are sold under the guise of making one "sexier." Of course, teenagers are obsessed with sex during their biological development, so it is easy for corporate America to pounce upon the fact that there is little parental mitigation in the child's life. Without adult mentors to explain the complexities of sexuality, corporations have taken on the role of sex teacher. Unfortunately, their message now, as it always has been, is "Buy more of it! Hurry! Don't worry!"

Aside from the systemic problems in the education world, we have already mentioned, our fundamental beliefs and foundations of the school are seriously flawed. We have based our system on the assumption that we in the West must prepare children for life in the workforce. "The idea that we're going to train a child at seven to get a good job at age twenty-seven is a travesty of profound dimension," states Joseph Chilton Pearce in an interview with *Wild Duck Review*. The economic control of the psyche in America has engendered economic control of the educational system. What children need is not a path chosen for them before birth, but a supportive culture in line with their own interests, physical and emotional development and evolutionary process—not to mention an education that is meant for their particular biological needs as boys and girls. The idea that boys and girls learn in the same way is as antique as the rotary dial telephone or the horse and buggy, yet we have based our schools upon it.

We have focused our education system on developing identity. Yet the identity that we encourage in the schools is not an individual identity; it is a common identity: worker, consumer, man, woman, follower of the status quo. This is a focus on the ego-self and on the brain's limbic-R-system alliance. Focusing all of our attention on the fulfillment and then reinforcement of this identity leaves little room for new ideas, new modes of learning or anything that may threaten or seem foreign to the identity which has already been constructed. In short, focusing the learning on the ancient brain prevents development that may take place in the neocortex and prefrontal lobes under the right conditions. We force the identification process on children and adolescents: "Are you a man or a mouse?" we ask them at age seven. "You need to decide whether you are going to be a good boy or a bad boy," we tell them around age ten. Or worse, we determine their identity for them, telling them what role in the consumer society they will fill, placing them in vocational courses at age fifteen or Advanced Placement courses in order to prepare them for their college study. Sometimes we simply tell them, "Your grandfather was a doctor, I am a doctor and you are going to become a doctor as well." Moreover, the electronic society has determined very narrow identities for boys and girls and the constant reinforcement of those roles in popular culture throughout childhood can be far more powerful than the parent's conversations, yet they are both building toward the same identity and sending the same message: be a consumer, value the physical world, deny the metaphysical and so on.

The horizontal society has repressed a great deal that could aid in educating our children. That which the communal psyche represses or refuses to acknowledge will smolder in the mind's dark places and some day come back to attack us with ferocious power. Carl Jung may have defined this idea, but modern psychology has at least accepted it, if not clarified it and studied it in depth. The idea of the repressed in our psyche is both a personal statement of psychological disorder and a comment about the dysfunctional communal psyche of organizations, cultures and nations in the modern era.

Looking at the horizontal society now, we can definitively say that the prevailing consciousness—those things we've discussed throughout this book, including the denial of art, the diminishment of language and communication, the abandonment of coming-of-age rituals, the perverse dismissal of mythology, the failure of American education, the embrace of the consumer society and the breakup of the American family—is the thing we are repressing in our communal minds. It is a repression that has grown in strength for some time, and a certain tipping point is either upon us now or is on the near horizon. One can only repress the important parts of the psyche for so long until great trouble rises to the surface. The proverbial Mr. Hyde dons his coat and top hat and starts patrolling the night streets, and horrible and terrifying things befall the culture.

Jung saw this in the individual as the "ego" being overwhelmed by the repression and suppression of other parts of the psyche. He viewed it, at least early in his career when he treated schizophrenics, often just after a psychotic episode had landed a patient in some sort of institution—just after Mr. Hyde had been let loose to do his business on the night streets.

The young have rebelled against the perceived threat of the elders and have reacted violently in places such as Somalia, Rwanda, Cambodia,

Sudan, Myanmar (Burma) and especially Germany and Eastern Europe during World War II. In what is now Cambodia, a powerful symbol of the youth's face of rebellion remains from the days of Pol-Pot and the Khmer Rouge. During the three years, eight months and twenty days of Pol-Pot's rule, "boy soldiers" spearheaded much of the torture and genocide that was committed against the Cambodian population. Today, one can visit the Tuol Sleng Genocide Museum on the outskirts of Phonm Penh. The site is a former school that was turned into a torture center during the dictator's reign. The classrooms were turned into detention cells with chains and shackles bolted to the walls and pillars. Detainees who were deemed to be a threat to the government, mainly people such as doctors, teachers, lawyers and other educated professionals, were tortured around the clock by the boy soldiers. They were beaten with sticks and branches, old broom handles or furniture legs, anything that was handy. When the boy soldiers tired of striking the prisoners, they took cigarette breaks and another group of boys took over the torture. This went on until the detainee confessed their involvement in the old regime. Once they confessed, the torture ceased and they were executed. If the boys were unable to extract a confession, the prisoners were beaten to death. Sometimes the boy soldiers wagered cigarettes on how long it would take the doctor or schoolmaster to die or whether they would be able to gain a confession from him. The boy soldiers were used all over the country during these years. It is estimated that between two and three million Cambodians were killed by the boy soldiers.

Such cases of large groups of young men rising up violently may result from the repressions and resentments their community harbored for so long. In Cambodia, as well as many of the other places where such atrocities occurred, youth culture took a very real resentment of the adult world and acted viciously upon it when the opportunity arose. Leaders such as Pol-Pot understood the festering repressions of his country's youth, their desperation and poverty, and took advantage of it to gain control of the nation. There are similar things happening today in Iraq, Afghanistan, Palestine, Darfur and elsewhere.

There is a long history of governments recruiting teenage boys to fight their wars for them. During World War I, thousands of boy soldiers were recruited into the British Army when Lord Kitchener waged a recruiting campaign that targeted teen patriotism. Children as young as twelve and thirteen were readily accepted into the military, even though the stated age for enlistment was nineteen. Hitler was also quite aware of the power of nationalism to motivate teenage boys. The 12th SS *Hitlerjugend* Panzer Division was made up mainly of teenagers, with 65 percent of the soldiers under age eighteen. Many of Hitler's elite soldiers came from Hitler Youth leadership schools, and it was not unusual to have fifteen and sixteen-year-olds fighting alongside adults in all areas of the German military.

The longing for identity, lack of compassion and inherent immaturity of teenage boys make them ideal targets for propaganda and indoctrination campaigns. The United Nations Children's Agency, UNICEF, is presently working with large numbers of boy soldiers from places like Sudan, Sierra Leone, Congo and Sri Lanka in order to return them to their families or relocate them as refugees. UNICEF, Save the Children and other international aid organizations have ongoing programs to demobilize, disarm and rehabilitate teenage soldiers from around the world. The Asian Regional Resource Center estimates that there are over 300,000 such boy soldiers currently fighting throughout the world. The problem seems to be at its worst in Burma, now called Myanmar. Here, there are estimated to be over 70,000 boy soldiers currently participating in either the state-run military or one of the many rebel groups.

Looking at the boy soldiers, the young Hamas suicide bombers, the teenage Taliban insurgents, the young men gunning down others on campuses, all convey that the face of male adolescence has grown weary of the adult world. They are rebelling, in the schools and in the streets, and the time has come to understand why this has occurred and what we can do to turn the anger around. We need to understand why male adolescents are no longer finding satisfactory identities in their homes or in their schools, and we need to make changes in both of these places to support and nurture our boys.

Conclusion

Parents need to know that without intervention, they are running a high risk of losing their sons by buying into the status quo. There are no longer reliable representatives of the adult community in schools, politics, churches or homes who will take our sons by the hand and lead them to meaningful adulthood. More than just an absence of adult leadership, there is an organized communication structure preaching a negative message to them and predators around nearly every corner. Worse still, the stories and mythology that created a pathway from childhood to adulthood have been tossed away. The adults need to forgo other considerations and retake the role of mentor and teacher from the television shows and performers. It will not happen quickly, nor will it happen easily. Many of our youths have already been lost, but there is still reason to hope.

It was no accident and no mistake that for so many thousands of years and across so many different geographies and cultures that a system of adults showing boys the way to adulthood developed. It happened because we have a deep and genetic predisposition to achieve a meaningful adulthood and an even deeper primal need to protect our children. If we see our role as adults as an act of saving our boys, then we might be able to do the hard work of saving them. Too many of us have believed for a long time that all is as it should be; that the world has become what it is because of forces beyond our control and that we are on a destructive path already predetermined. But real adults do not think this way. Real adults know that they can lead, that they can make change, that they can touch others and change their lives. This belief is the foundation of vertical development. I believe we can still reach higher, even if it means abandoning some of the cultural pillars we now embrace.

Like the William Stafford poem I used to share with my students on the last day of school reminds us:

> and as elephants parade holding each elephant's tail,
> but if one wanders the circus won't find the park,

and

> though we could fool each other, we should consider—
> lest the parade of our mutual life get lost in the dark.
> The signals we give—yes or no, or maybe—
> should be clear: the darkness around us is deep.

So what should a culture do if they have metaphorically wandered, taken a wrong turn and are now "lost in the dark?" Well, the first step is to examine what went wrong. Some of the things I've pointed out in this book are clues to where our mutual lives went astray. We should look even further back for models as well; before the American paternal culture and back to the indigenous cultures in North America and around the world. These were cultures that lived for many generations and successfully raised boys to adulthood throughout.

We should also look at life through the eyes of our boys. What do they see when they turn on the television, when they come home from school to an empty house, when they need the support and guidance of a mother and father who are not there? If we can see through their eyes, we can empathize; if we can rekindle empathy, we can then teach empathy, and that will be the start of solving our problem. Empathy is a slippery concept, but fundamental to growing adult humanity. If one can see and experience the suffering of others, we can then be motivated to act. If a child can empathize, he will develop an "interior judge" that guides in self-regulation and the agencies of self-control that will steer him away from violence and underachievement. In our culture we are trained to deny personal and communal failure, but what we need is an examination of these failures and a deep study of the past successes of the people, tribes and artists who once knew of the way to vertical achievement.

In Western countries since about 1850 or so, too many fathers have become dispossessed, and male children have become the desirable model. In the large picture, this showed a tremendous ingratitude to the fathers who came before, and an even larger insult to mothers, who were already subjugated in the paternal model. We have reached a point where our ancestors have become unimportant. The arrogance of this paradigm is tremendous.

We now realize there are no perfect parents and no perfect children. We also know that raising boys in today's culture is difficult without somehow damaging their psyches, their sense of self-worth and their compassion. We also know that it has become more difficult to support a boy who can develop vertically, reach for higher achievement, deeper knowledge and real psychic growth. It seems that even parents who realize the need for a nurturing mythology, community support and parental proximity are fighting a losing battle with omnipresent cultural forces.

I began writing this book because I was working with so many young boys in the classroom whom I thought of as being wounded or lost. Many went home to parentless households, abuse, violence, drugs, distraction, indifference. Theirs was a painful adolescence I sensed they would never emerge from. I would hand out a short story to a class of twenty-five students, tell them that they must read it carefully, answer the questions that followed and, most of all, try and focus, because this was a test. Time after time, two or three, or maybe five of the students would undertake the task. But a majority of the kids either couldn't read the material, couldn't comprehend it, were too distracted to complete the task or just didn't care enough to put any effort forth. Too many of the teenagers spent their time on writing notes, sleeping, cursing, picking their noses—anything but literacy. The same was true for trying to give them creative assignments to do as it was for prescribed curriculum. My colleagues in the Math and Science departments had experienced the same indifference. It made me believe that many children, especially boys, were not just unprepared for the task at hand, but they were truly unprepared to learn anything.

Nevertheless, even while this is going on in our schools, some boys still endeavor to make it to the best colleges and pursue their academic and professional dreams. But a lot of boys are now seeing other ways to become successful. The media trains them regularly that to be "one of us" you must be part of the consumer culture. They are being offered more opportunities than ever to join. At the upscale coffee shop near my home, the store manager is a sixteen-year-old who oversees a staff of fifteen employees, yet is too young to drive. The consumer culture values youth over experience. The average age of a corporate CEO in America has come down eleven years since 1950 to forty-eight years old.

Our cultural icons are mostly adolescent superstar athletes and entertainers—Shaun White in snowboarding, LeBron James in basketball, Chris Brown in music—and all have their respective multi-million dollar endorsement deals to match. We have either turned our culture over to the children or we have remained children—or at least child-like ourselves. The United Nations Convention on the Rights of the Child urges that children's views and opinions be taken into account by society's authority. Note the language: we are to take into account their *opinions*, not their best interests. Academics around the country, such as Claire Cassidy with *Childhood & Philosophy*, are presently presenting papers advocating the need for "younger members of society to partake in their role as citizens." The hierarchy of the paternal culture and the mythological guidance of traditional and indigenous cultures have disappeared in one click of the television age, and we are now scrambling to make sense of the role of children in a world with fewer and fewer hierarchies—a world where the children lead the children.

A Final Story

In the Grimm Brothers' fairy tale *Godfather Death*, a poor father is searching for someone to be godfather for his new son. The pitiable tailor has thirteen children, and he has determined that he can no longer feed his brood. Desperate, he runs out to the road seeking anyone who can help feed his newborn son. First to pass along the road is God. Seeing Him, the tailor shrivels and turns away. His economic suffering is so great, and his lot so difficult, he sees God as cruel. "God gives to the rich and takes from the poor," he thinks. "I'll wait for the next person to come." But the next to pass along the desolate road is the Devil. The tailor rejects him as well. "The Devil lies and cheats and leads the good astray," he deduces. "I'll wait for another." But it is growing late, and soon enough the last traveler of the evening comes by. This traveler is Death, and the poor tailor contemplates his presence carefully. "At least Death treats all men as equals," reasons the tailor. "I will ask him to be my son's godfather." Death readily agrees.

As the years pass, Godfather Death is indeed a kind guide. He makes sure the family wants nothing, and as the boy grows to become a man, he asks his godfather for help. "I will give you what you need to be the greatest doctor in the land," Godfather Death offers. He gives the boy a secret medicine to use with his patients, and also some advice: "If you see me standing at the end of the patient's bed, you will know that he is going to die. If not, then you can give him the medicine and accurately predict that he will recover. Your diagnosis will always be right."

With these gifts, the young man becomes a famous healer and a confidante of the king himself. When the king falls ill, he summons the young doctor to his bedside. But upon arrival, the doctor sees that the king is quite ill and that Death is standing at the foot of his bed. Acting quickly, the doctor turns the bed around, pours some of the magic medicine into his mouth and cures him. Later, Godfather Death warns, "You must never cheat me again! If you do, it will be all over for you."

But the young doctor does not learn. Sometime later, the king's only daughter falls ill and the doctor is summoned to the castle once again. The king's daughter is slender and beautiful, with skin like soft lotion, and the doctor falls immediately in love with her. But once again, upon surveying the room, he sees Death standing at the foot of her bed, waiting to take her. "Please," pleads the king. "Save her life! Save her life!"

Heartsick, the doctor turns the bed away from death and pours the magic medicine into her mouth, curing her.

In an instant, Godfather Death grabs the doctor with his bony fingers and takes him away to his cave. There, he shows the young man millions of burning candles lining the walls of the cave, one for every person on earth. "This one is yours," says Death, pointing to a candle whose wick has burned down so that only a small pool of wax remains. "Please Godfather," begs the godson. "Please light another candle for me." But Death gazes at him coldly. The candle flickers out and the young man falls dead on the floor of the cave.

It might seem that some of the stories in this book show modern parents to be cold-hearted, unfeeling, uncaring, absent or abusive toward their sons. Certainly, there are some parents like this. But I don't think that as a society we lack love for our boys. I don't think that is the problem at all. Instead, we have carefully considered the options for what we are able to give to them. Much like the father in the Grimms' story, many in the post-modern generations feel communally tired, overwhelmed and overburdened—perhaps even desperate. Like the doctor's father, I believe we have few choices, and all of them are quite problematic.

Today, then, our options for educating boys are scanty. Unless we are unusually wealthy, we must send them to the public school assigned by their local board. In many cases, it is a place of high-stakes testing, high-stress and it is dominated by a prevailing pragmatic attitude that dismisses the arts, philosophy, critical thinking, anything other than what will deliver economic satisfaction. We must consider that this approach may be changing the evolutionary pattern of childhood development, or perhaps, combined with the bombardment of television during early childhood, may have stopped it altogether.

For similar reasons, too many parents have handed over the responsibility of parenting, raising and mentoring our children to a suite of technologies run by a corporate mega-machine. Television's prominence in children's lives is undeniable, and its negative effect on brain biology and behavioral outcomes needs to be seriously studied. Even I, a caring parent who has deeply researched the destructive effects of technology on children, turn on the television occasionally. My children play on computers at school. My two-year-old is already reaching for the computer mouse on my desk. It is easy to feel as though technology, pragmatism and the horizontal mind are omnipotent. But they are not.

It is not too late to take back control of our children. Many people all over the world are beginning to understand that something has gone very wrong. Organizations are forming, parents are banding together and teachers are organizing to fight against the negative forces. Now *we* need to take action. We must remake our schools, our culture and secure for our children promising futures.

Bibliography

Alan Guttmacher Institute, The. *Sex and America's Teenagers.* New York: Alan Guttmacher Institute, 1994.

American Social Health Association. *Sexually Transmitted Diseases in America: How Many Cases and at What Cost?* Kaiser Family Foundation, December 1998.

Anderson, Craig A. and Brad J. Bushman. "Effects of violent video games on aggressive behavior, aggressive cognition, aggressive affect, physiological arousal, and prosocial behavior: A meta-analytic review of the scientific literature." *Psychological Science* 12 (September 2001): 353.

Asian Regional Resource Center, The. *End the Use of Children as Soldiers in Burma.* The Asian Regional Resource Center, November 2003.

Astor, Susan. "Sea People." *Silent Voices: Recent American Poems about Nature.* Ed. Paul Feroe. St. Paul: Ally Press, 1978.

Bly, Robert. *The Sibling Society.* Reading, MA: Addison-Wesley Publishing Company, 1996.

Bauder, David. "Almost Unnoticed, Prime-Time TV Becomes the Place for Blood 'n' Guts." *Associated Press.* New York: Associated Press, 20 November 2005. Copyright: The Canadian Press, 2005.

Bowman-Kruhn, Mary. *Margaret Mead: A Biography.* Greenwood Press, 2003.

Campbell, Joseph and Bill Moyers. *The Power of Myth*. New York: Doubleday, 1988.

Cassidy, Claire. "Child and Community of Philosophical Inquiry." *Childhood & Philosophy: A Journal of the International Council of Philosophical Inquiry with Children* vol. 2 no. 4 (2006).

Centers for Disease Control and Prevention. "School Health Guidelines to Prevent Unintentional Injuries and Violence." *Morbidity and Mortality Weekly Report* vol. 50 no. RR22 (7 December 2001).

Changeux, Jean-Pierre. *L'Homme Neuronal*. Fayard: Paris, 1983.

Christakis, Dimitri A., Frederick J. Zimmerman, David L. DiGiuseppe and Carolyn A. McCarty. "Early Television Exposure and Subsequent Attentional Problems in Children." *Pediatrics*, vol. 113, no. 4 (April 2004): 708-713.

Clemetson, Lynette. "Parents Making Use of TV Despite Risks," *The New York Times*, 25 May 2006.

Congressional Public Health Summit (26, July 2000). Joint statement on the impact of entertainment violence on children. Accessed at: www.aap.org/advocacy/releases/jstmtevc.htm (last visited 2/14/02)

Council on Contemporary Families. *Stereotypes Versus Statistics: Data on America's Changing Families*. Council on Contemporary Families, 26 January 2006. http://www.contemporaryfamilies.org/subtemplate.php?t=education&ext=stereotypesedu

Curtin, Jeremiah. *Myths and Folklore of Ireland*. (Boston, Little, and Brown, 1899). Quoted in Padraic Colum, *Great Myths of the World* (Dover Publications, 2005).

Dawkins, Richard. *The Ancestor's Tale*. Houghton Mifflin, 2004.

Dickens, Charles. *A Child's Story*. 1852.

Eddy, Steve. *Native American Myths*. Contemporary Books, 2001.

Eddy, Steve and Claire Hamilton. "Greek Myths." 2008. www.livingmyths.com/Greek.htm

Fair, Charles. *The Dying Self*. Wesleyan University Press, 1969.

Fauconnier, Gilles and Mark Turner. *The Way We Think: Conceptual Blending and the Mind's Hidden Complexities*. New York: Basic Books, 2002.

Frontline: The Merchants of Cool, prod. Barak Goodman and Rachel Dretzin, 60 min., WGBH Educational Foundation, distributed by PBS, 2001.

Gentile, Douglas; Walsh, David A.; Ellison, Paul R.; Fox, Michelle; Cameron, Jennifer. *Media Violence as a Risk Factor for Children: A Longitudinal Study*. Paper Presented at the American Psychological Society 16th Annual Convention, Chicago, IL. May, 2004.

Gere, Anne Ruggles, Colleen Fairbanks, Alan Howes, Laura Roop and David Schaafsma. *Language and Reflection: An Integrated Approach to Teaching English*. New York: Prentice Hall, 1992.

Gootman, Elissa. "High School Graduation Rates Unacceptably Low, State Says." *The New York Times*. 14 February 2006.

Graves, Robert. *The Greek Myths*. New York: Penguin. 1969.

Grimm, Jacob and Wilhelm Grimm. "Godfather Death." *Children's and Household Tales*. 1857.

Gurian, Michael and Kathy Stevens. *The Minds of Boys: Saving Our Sons from Falling Behind in School and Life*. San Francisco: Jossey-Bass, 2005.

Hamilton, Virginia. *In The Beginning: Creation Stories from Around the World*. New York: Harcourt, Brace, Jovanovich, 1988.

Hawkins, J. David, T.I. Herrenkohl, D.P. Farrington, D. Brewer, R.F. Catalano, T.W. Harachi and L. Cothern. "Predictors of Youth Violence." *Juvenile Justice Bulletin* (April 2000)

Henshaw, S. K. *U.S. Teenage Pregnancy Statistics with Comparative Statistics for Women 20-24*, New York: The Alan Guttmacher Institute, 2003.

Heyen, William. "On an Archaic Torso of Apollo (after Rilke)." *The Swastika Poems*. New York, NY: The Vanguard Press, 1977.

Heyen, William, ed. *The Generation of 2000: Contemporary American Poets*. Ontario Review Press, 1984.

Heyen, William. "The Pigeons." *Pterodactyl Rose: Poems of Ecology*. St. Louis, MO: Time Being Books, 1991.

Highwater, Jamake. *The Primal Mind*. New American Library, 1981.

Hollich, G., R. Newman and P. Jusczyk. "Infants' Use of Synchronized Visual Information to Separate Streams of Speech." *Child Development* vol. 76, no. 3 (May/June 2005) 598-613.

Homer. *The Odyssey*. 800 B.C.E

Huttenlocher, P. R. "Dendritic and Synaptic Development in Human Cerebral Cortex: Time Course and Critical Periods." *Developmental Neuropsychology* vol. 16, no. 3 (1999) 347-349.

Jacobs, Andrew. "Cadaver Exhibition Raises Questions Beyond Taste." *New York Times.* 18 November 2005.

Jung, Carl. "The Basic Postulates of Analytical Psychology." In *Modern Man in Search of a Soul,* trans. by Cary Baynes. Routledge & Kegan Paul, 1933.

Katz, Albert, Cristina Cacciari, Ray Gibbs, Jr. and Mark Turner. *Figurative Language and Thought.* New York: Oxford University Press, 1998.

Kelly, Howard. *Gynecology.* New York: D. Appleton and Company, 1928.

Lakoff, George and Mark Turner. *More than Cool Reason: a Field Guide to Poetic Metaphor.* Chicago: University of Chicago Press, 1989.

Lewin, Roger. "Is the Brain Really Necessary?" *Science* vol. 210, no. 4475 (December 1980): 1232-1234.

MacLean, Paul D. "A Triune Concept of the Brain and Behavior." In *The Hincks Memorial Lectures* by D. Campbell and T.J. Boag, ed. Toronto: University of Toronto Press, 1973.

Marriott, Alice, and Carol K. Rachlin. *American Indian Mythology.* New York: Crowell, 1968.

McGrath, Ellen. "Teen Depression—Girls." *Psychology Today: Blues Buster,* 1 June 2002.

Neighmond, Patti. "'Generation Next' in the Slow Lane to Adulthood." *National Public Radio: Morning Edition.* 20 December 2007. http://www.npr.org/templates/story/story.php?storyId=17429734

Nelson, Richard K. *Make Prayers to the Raven: A Koyukon View of the Northern Forest.* University of Chicago Press, 1983.

Neruda, Pablo. *Canto General.* Trans. James Wright. Debolsillo, 2004.

Nossel, Ilana. "Pregnancy and Childbearing Among Younger Teens." *Uncovering the Facts About Adolescent Sexual Health.* Advocates for Youth, October 1996.

Olson, James S. and Raymond Wilson. *Native Americans in the 20th Century.* University of Illinois Press, 1984.

Pearce, Joseph Chilton. *Evolution's End: Claiming the Potential of Our Intelligence.* San Francisco: Harper, 1992.

—. "An Interview with Joseph Chilton Pearce." Interview by Chris Mercogliano and Kim Debus. *Journal of Family Life*, vol. 5, no. 1 (1999).

—. "Waking Up to the Holographic Heart: Starting Over with Education." Interview by Casey Walker. *Wild Duck Review*, vol. IV, no. 2 (1998).

Postman, Neil. *Amusing Ourselves to Death. Public Discourse in the Age of Show Business.* New York, NY: Viking Penguin, 1985.

—. "Informing Ourselves to Death." The German Informatics Society. Stuttgart, Germany, 11 October 1990.

Proctor, Jennifer. "Medical School Debt: Making Sense of Life in the Red." *AAMC Reporter* vol. 9, no. 6 (March 2000).

Rahaman, Vashanti. "The Man Who Could See Elephants." *Highlights for Children*, 1 October 2002.

Raphael, Ray. *The Men from the Boys: Rites of Passage in Male America.* University of Nebraska Press, 1988.

Romano, Lois. "Literacy of College Graduates is on Decline." *Washington Post*, 25 December 2005.

Rumi. "Ecstatic Love is an Ocean." In *The Winged Energy of Delight: Selected Translations, Poems from Europe, Asia and the Americas*. Ed. Robert Bly. New York: Harper Collins, 2005.

Ryan, R.M., E.L. Deci, W.S. Grolnick and J.G. La Guardia (in press). "The significance of autonomy and autonomy support in psychological development and psychopathology." In D. Cicchetti & D. Cohen, eds., *Developmental Psychopathology, Vol. 1: Theory and Method (snd ed.)*. New Jersey: John Wiley & Sons, Inc.

Ryan, R.M., J.G. La Guardia, J. Solky-Butzel, V. Chirkov and Y. Kim. (2005). "On the interpersonal regulation of emotions: Emotional reliance across gender, relationships and cultures." *Personal Relationships*, 12, 145-163.

Ryan, R.M. & Deci, E.L. (2004). Autonomy is No Illusion: Self-Determination Theory and the Empirical Study of Authenticity, Awareness and Will. In J. Greenberg, S.L. Koole & T. Pyszcynski (Eds.) Greenberg, Jeff, Sander Leon Koole and Thomas A. Pyszczynski. *Handbook of Experimental Existential Psychology.* New York: Guilford Press, 2004. (pp. 449-479).

Sale, Kirkpatrick. *Rebels Against the Future*. Reading, MA: Addison-Wesley Publishing Company, 1995.

Smith, S. L., & E. Donnerstein. "Harmful effects of exposure to media violence: Learning of aggression, emotional desensitization, and fear." (1998) In R. G. Geen & E. Donnerstein, eds., *Human Aggression: Theories, Research and Implications for Social Policy* (New York: Academic Press, 1998), 167-202.

Stanford, Barbara. "'Somebody Died?' Using Grammar to Construct Meaning in Adolescent Literature." *English Journal* vol. 95, no. 5 (May 2006): 60.

Thomas, Francis-Noël Thomas and Mark Turner. *Clear and Simple as the Truth: Writing Classic Prose*. Princeton, New Jersey: Princeton University Press, 1994.

Turner, Mark. *Cognitive Dimensions of Social Science: The Way We Think About Politics, Economics, Law and Society*. New York: Oxford University Press, 2001.

—-. *The Literary Mind: The Origins of Language and Thought*. New York: Oxford University Press, 1996.

—-. *Reading Minds: The Study of English in the Age of Cognitive Science*. Princeton, New Jersey: Princeton University Press, 1991.

—-. *Death is the Mother of Beauty: Mind, Metaphor, Criticism*. Chicago: University of Chicago Press, 1987.

Tyre, Peg. "The Trouble with Boys." *Newsweek*. 30 January 2006.

Walsh, David, Douglas Gentile, Erin Walsh, Nat Bennett, Brad Robideau, Monica Walsh, Sarah Strickland and David McFadden. "Tenth Annual MediaWise® Video Game Report Card." *National Institute on Media and the Family*. 29 November 2005.

Weiner, Eric. "Why Women Read More than Men." *National Public Radio*. 5 September 2007.
http://www.npr.org/templates/story/story.php?storyId=14175229

Whitman, Walt. "Song of Myself." *Leaves of Grass*. 1855, 1892.